Artdolls

Basic Sculpting and Beyond

Artdolls

BASIC SCULPTING AND BEYOND

Jack Johnston

Portfolio Press

First edition/First printing

To purchase additional copies of this book, please contact:
Portfolio Press, 130 Wineow Street, Cumberland, MD 21502
877-737-1200

Library of Congress Control Number 2002116607
ISBN 0-942620-67-4

Project Editor: Krystyna Poray Goddu
Design & Production: Tammy S. Blank
Cover design by John Vanden-Heuvel Design
Photography by Jack Johnston and Ron Boswell
Photo composition, page 2, by Rebecca Summers

Printed and bound in Korea

Dedication

Few people have ever achieved anything by themselves; my career is no different. Throughout the beginning years of my newfound career, I received tremendous support from many wonderful people. Those that stand out are Senator Paula Hawkins, Mr. and Mrs. Phillip Crosby, Danny and Barry Shapiro of The Toy Shoppe, Richard and Peter Bell of Bell Ceramics, Bob and Ruth Keessen of Scott Publications, Handcraft Designs, Bob and Jane Poole (my mother and stepfather) and, of course, my wife, Vicky. Further support came from my students, friends in the industry and the professional artists with whom I associate. It is with their support and encouragement that I have been able to achieve much of the success I have enjoyed.

There is one nameless person I would like to thank, too. Many years ago, after I was laid off from my job, I spent some months out of work. We quickly went through the few dollars we had in savings and found it very difficult to feed our six children. One day while shopping for bargains at one of the local grocery stores, I saw the butcher throwing away twenty pounds of hamburger, just because it was turning brown. I told him I didn't have a job and that I could sure use that meat to feed my family. He said, "Even though the meat is still perfectly good I have to throw it out by law." He saw that I was serious and asked, "Are you willing to work?" I said, "absolutely," and he instructed me: "Come by the store Saturday morning at six, and I'll put you to work."

Saturday morning I showed up right on time and reported to the butcher for my first assignment. He said, "I have these packages that need to be thrown out." There were four very neatly wrapped five-pound packages of hamburger marked "day old…dispose" sitting on the back counter. He said, "I want you to carry these packages out through the back door and dispose of them. That's all I have for you to do this week, but I want you to come back every Saturday until you find a job." I didn't have to ask twice how or where I was to dispose of them; I just did what he asked me to do. I still can't tell this story without breaking down in tears. I don't know his name and he likely wouldn't want me to tell it even if I could because of the liability implications. To me, he was a saint; giving me the food when I needed it so badly was a gift from heaven. So whoever you are, "thanks, you made a difference in our lives."

Therefore, it is with gratitude that I dedicate this writing to my friends, fellow artists, my family and the butcher. Many of the ideas and concepts in this book came as a result of listening and learning from others. Together we accomplish far greater feats than we ever do alone, and in a considerably shorter time. Helping others has become a way for me to repay society for the great things it has done for me. I shall never forget the kindness that was given to me during my time of need. Thank you, my dear friends.

—Jack Johnston

Contents

If you have a dream to achieve, you will. If your dream is strong enough, you will achieve greatly.

When you share your dreams, they will last forever.

— Jack Johnston

Foreword

by Marie Osmond

I first met Jack Johnston in 1991 at the Walt Disney World Doll and Teddy Bear Convention in Orlando. We were both new to the world of dollmaking and, both being from Utah, we had something in common.

Over the years we became friends. For the past ten years we have each had our respective doll booths at the American International Toy Fair in New York City every February, and at other shows around the nation. Along with building his doll business, Jack has made a wonderful contribution to the industry and to his fellow artists.

As the founder and Chairman of the Board of the nonprofit Professional Doll Makers Art Guild (PDMAG), Jack has been responsible for bringing hundreds of burgeoning artists into this wonderful industry. As he brings them to shows around the country, I've had the opportunity to meet some of them. Many of the artists have become quite successful and several have made their way to the top of the industry.

Through Jack's leadership, the Professional Doll Makers Art Guild has contributed thousands of dollars to The Children's Miracle Network (CMN), of which I am one of the founders. CMN raises much-needed funds for children's hospitals all throughout North America. The PDMAG's artists donate scores of their dolls each year to charity. This sharing attitude has become part of the mission of the PDMAG and its artists.

The first doll I sculpted was with Jack in one of his dollmaking seminars. His seminars, writings and videos have become the dollmaking foundation for thousands of artists. I'm proud to call Jack Johnston a friend. I'm sure you will learn and benefit from reading this book, and getting to know him. If you study these dollmaking techniques closely and catch the same vision Jack has toward helping others, they can help you develop the skills necessary to reach your potential and be a contributor to the wonderful world of dollmaking.

A Note to My Readers and Fellow Artists

Jack Johnston, at age 16, sculpts a self portrait.

As a dollmaker, I have spent a large portion of my adult life creating the dreams and visions that have been captured in my head since my youth. I vividly remember, as a young boy, studying carefully the illustrations of Norman Rockwell reproduced on the covers of the *Saturday Evening Post* magazine. While other children were playing baseball, I was drawing characters after Mr. Rockwell's illustrations.

Sculpting dolls can be highly rewarding, both emotionally and financially, but it is only a tiny piece of the complete dollmaking process. Making the dolls come to life and helping them tell a story is the challenge of all dollmakers. It is tremendously gratifying to see your dreams come to fruition with the completion of a doll. There is a special feeling of creation that comes over artists as we labor over our own works. As

an educator, I admire the works of my students and fellow artists. The satisfaction of seeing one of my students achieve greatly in the doll world is as much of a thrill as doing it myself.

If we make dolls for our own edification or for the enjoyment of our friends then it is relatively easy to reach a level of satisfaction. On the other hand, if we have chosen to make dolls as a profession, then our work is a continuing process of practicing, studying and promoting our dollmaking effort. Once a person has accomplished the skill of making wonderful dolls, there is another step that lurks just out of reach for most dollmakers: the constantly alluring marketplace.

I have spent my life working as a marketer in one form or another. I was born with a "gift of gab," which makes it easy for me to talk to others. In many ways,

Jack Johnston, at age 56, sculpts the Aviator.

Norman Rockwell (Photo ©William H. Tague)

marketing and the ability to sell products of value comes naturally to me. If this is the case for you, then you are fortunate, too. However, if you are like most artists, you may not like to talk to others about purchasing your creations.

As a professional artdoll maker, I think of the eventual consumer from the very moment I form the armature that serves as the foundation for my piece. For me, it isn't enough to enjoy making dolls for myself; I consider the collectors' likes and dislikes far above my own desires. After all, it is the end user that keeps artists in business.

There is a fine line between what we like to sculpt as artists and what the consumers will purchase. We have learned a great deal about what gets the most attention at doll shows and exhibitions around the world. It seems all shows are much the same. The first doll to sell is always a baby doll, followed by children, beautiful ladies, character dolls, Christmas figures and

then religious figures. With this experience in mind, I have made it my goal in this book to not only teach you the rudiments of sculpting and making a doll, but I will try to direct you on the proper course to making a creation that will sell. If you choose to pass your work on to a collector or a doll enthusiast, following some of the tips in this book may be of help to you.

I have another compelling reason for writing this book. When I was a beginning sculptor, I found an annoying lack of support in the dollmaking industry for helping one another. I came to dollmaking directly after spending 25 years as a marketer in the resort industry. The business world taught me the value of sharing ideas with one another through marketing conventions, publications, educational videos and workshops. Every symposium I attended in those 25 years stressed the importance of sharing our knowledge to promote growth and perpetuate our business. My first impression of dollmakers was that artists lacked the willingness to share their ideas and techniques with beginners. For some unknown reason, many wanted to keep the craft to themselves; it was almost as though sculpting dolls was a trade secret.

Everyone has the right to express himself or herself as an artist; anyone who desires to become a dollmaker can do so. The extent to which anyone achieves greatness is relative to his or her personal goals and to the amount of effort one is willing to contribute. All dolls are wonderful; some are just better than others are. Therefore, this book is written to encourage all those desiring to improve their skills as dollmakers. Never be discouraged if your work isn't exactly what you want, just continue to practice and study. Time and practice will improve your skills to the level at which you feel satisfied and complete as an artist. Whether you are sculpting for your own enjoyment or as a profession, the rudiments of the task are exactly the same.

Most polymer dolls are made by the same method: hand sculpted, with cloth bodies and fabric costumes. If they are all made using much the same techniques, then what is the difference between a doll sculpted by a master that sells for thousands of dollars and one sculpted by a beginner that is sometimes hard to give away? The only difference is the skill level in the hands of the artist. What makes the master so much better than the beginning sculptor? The answer can be given in three words, "practice, practice, practice." With practice and study you can be a master sculptor, too. Of course, some people have a natural talent. For them, mastering the craft is easier than for others; nonetheless, there is a learning curve that everyone has to go through. It seems reasonable to believe that if you are reading this book you have some natural talent, or at least a strong desire, therefore I am convinced you can do it. This book is dedicated to showing you the steps to sculpting a doll and should help motivate you to see your own potential. It is important to know from the start, however, that your first doll may not be as good as you would like it to be. But by following the simple steps in this book, you will be able to make a presentable doll and you will learn the skills to continue practicing this wonderful trade. Historically, I have found that if a person is willing to stay with their sculpting until they have completed 20 dolls, they will make it in the dollmaking industry. If you are making dolls for your own amusement, then your first few will be exciting and rewarding. If you wish to make them for your friends and family, you can expect to amaze them after the first three or four. If you plan to supplement your income by selling dolls, expect to make at least ten before you have a marketable doll. If your desire is to make a living making dolls, don't quit your day job until you have practiced for at least two years and have made at least 20 dolls. By the time you have paid your dues and made the prescribed sculptures, you will know if you're ready to sell your work full time.

All the above is why I say don't expect too much out of your first sculpture. Stay with it, don't judge yourself, or ask anyone else to judge your work, until you have finished at least ten dolls. New students forget that growing accomplished at anything takes time. If you were learning to play the piano, you wouldn't give up the first time you tried. You might have to practice for months before you felt confident to play for your friends. You wouldn't even think of being paid for your music until you had practiced and rehearsed for years. The same is true for dollmaking. Hildegard Gunzel, one of the world's most popular artists, practiced 15 years before she was commercially successful. Liberace, one of the most famous pianists of the 20th century, practiced every day of his life until the day he died.

Students often ask: when will I know if my work is good enough to be sold? It's really very simple: while exhibiting your work, watch people's eyes and listen to their comments when you tell them the price. The answer to "when am I ready?" is "when collectors start purchasing your work."

CHAPTER 1

Tools, Supplies and Materials

Sculpting with polymer clay can be done anywhere and with very few tools. Making artdolls of polymer clay is one of the least expensive methods of making dolls. Even though it requires a few specialized tools to make polymer dolls, these are not expensive. One of the major advantages of polymer clay is that it can be cured in a household oven. When you travel, you may cure the clay in a toaster oven. The following list of supplies, materials, equipment and tools will help you in preparing to sculpt your creations.

Sculpting tools

Sculpting tools are quite simple; they may be especially hand made, they may be dental tools or simply pieces of wood or plastic fashioned by the user. Any tool that fits your hand well and feels good to you will work as a sculpting tool. There are however, tools available that make sculpting much easier. The sculpting tool that I recommend most is one that I created some years ago, which I call the 3-1 tool.

After I designed the prototype for this tool, I contacted the Kemper Tool Company and asked them to manufacture it for me. They obliged, and it is now sold as the Kemper/Johnston Primary Sculpting Tool. The advantages of it are that it is three tools in one. The primary sculpting tool is on one end. The other end has a tool for sculpting ears. On the back of the ear tool is a tool for sculpting fingernails. This tool is designed

specifically for making polymer dolls ranging in size from 14-24 inches tall. For dolls larger than 24 inches, you will need a larger tool, and of course, for dolls smaller than 14 inches, you will need smaller tools.

Top: The Kemper/Johnston primary sculpting tool is three tools in one. Above: The close-up view shows the primary sculpting tool on the left and the ear tool on the right. The fingernail tool is on the obverse side of the ear tool.

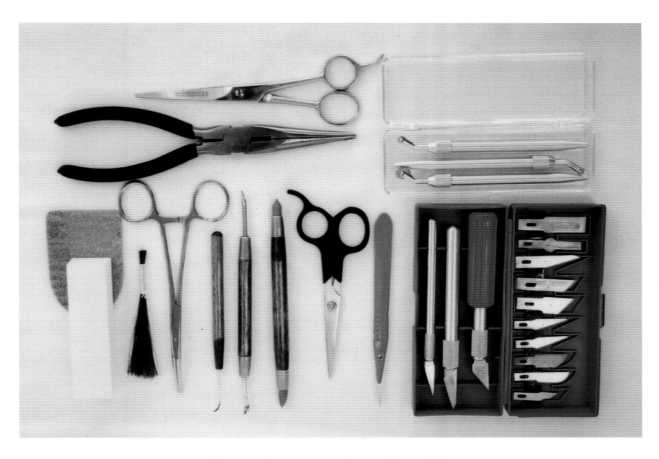

Following is a list of the tools and materials needed to complete a polymer doll.

- Polymer clay, flesh color: at least one pound
- Polymer clay, translucent white, for teeth and fingernails: two ounces
- Glass, porcelain or silicon eyes (See page 15 for guidance as to the appropriate size and color)
- Head armature, or aluminum foil to make your own armature: use one foot of foil for every inch of the head's height. For example, a three-inch head will need a three-foot piece of foil.
- Hand armature
- Body stocking and body armature
- One bag of Polyfill
- Mohair, for hair (See pages 16-18 for guidance as to appropriate color, texture and amount)
- Sculpting tool, made of stainless steel, plastic or wood
- Detail tool, with a small point for making wrinkles on the face and lines on the shoes
- Hemostat (eight inches long) for making the hands and stuffing the body
- Needle-nose pliers
- Horsehair brush for wrinkles around eyes of old people
- Soft-sculpting needle, three inches

- Upholstery thread, matched to the color of your body stocking
- Disappearing-ink pen for making patterns of the body stocking and costume
- One medium-weight sanding block, such as those used for porcelain dollmaking
- One fine sanding disk, such as those used for filing acrylic fingernails
- Hot Glue with additional sticks
- Fabri-Tac glue and super glue
- Acrylic paint: one small tube or bottle, of each of the following colors: Cadmium Red, Mars Black, Burnt Sienna, Raw Umber and Unbleached Titanium
- Lacquer thinner, or acetone
- Acrylic paintbrushes: eyeliner, lip brush, mop brush, detailer, #9 flat bristle brush
- Cotton swabs (The best are those that come to a point for detail work in small places.)
- Paper towels
- Household oven or a large toaster oven

Good lighting is essential. If you don't have adequate lighting, I recommend purchasing an all-spectrum desk lamp, which ensures that you will get accurate colors when you paint. If you paint under florescent lighting, your paints will have a tendency to follow the green hues.

Most of these tools and supplies may be found at art and craft stores, dollmaking shops or on the internet. Chain stores such as Michael's, Hobby Lobby, and Pearl Craft Stores carry nearly everything you need. Some tools and supplies are so difficult to find that you need to go to a shop or web site specializing in one-of-a-kind dolls. (See Sources on page 143).

Polymer clay

The methods that I write about in this book will work for any of the polymer clays on the market. I recommend, however, that you use a clay with the ASTM D-4236 Non-Toxic label. For a clay to be approved for use in the United States, it must carry a Non-Toxic label from The Art and Creative Materials Institute (ACMI). This organization carefully tests each of the clays and creative materials that are sold for crafts within the United States. Upon the successful completion of laboratory testing, each of the products receives a label stating that the product is non-toxic and that it conforms to the standards of the testing criteria. The products that have been tested and approved have the following code

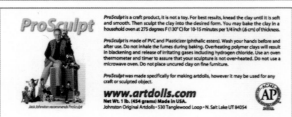

printed on their labels, "ASTM D-4236." This indicates that the clay and other creative materials tested are deemed safe to use under normal conditions.

Polymer clay is non-allergenic, non-toxic and safe for home craft use, however there are two conditions that I caution users about. First, never overheat polymer clay to the point that it turns black or burns. Under extreme heat (approximately 400 degrees), it starts to bubble in the oven and turn black. If the temperature is not lowered, the clay will eventually burn. Therefore, I recommend that you follow the instructions on the back of the package of clay and do not exceed the recommended curing times and temperatures (ten to fifteen minutes at 275 degrees C or 30 degrees F). If you accidentally overheat the oven, you may cause fumes that pollute the air in your work area. If this happens, you should open windows and vent the area, trying not to breathe in the fumes.

Second, even though there is no written proof that breathing the sanding dust from polymer clay is harmful, I recommend that you wear a safety facemask or sand the clay under water. I prefer to sand the clay under water as that completely eliminates any sanding dust and it allows the sanding pad to do a better job of sanding. This may be done under running water from a faucet in the sink. Such a small amount of dried clay is sanded that it won't hurt to wash it down the drain.

I have personally used all of the clays that have been tested and passed by the ACMI Institute. They all work very much the same, and for the most part all are made from the same ingredients. Some clays are very hard; others are very soft. The difference between the clays is due to the amount of plasticiser, polyvinyl chloride, and silicon that they have in their respective formulas. Choose whichever brand of polymer clay you like best. All of these work well with the methods I suggest in this book. The polymer clays that I recommend are: ProSculpt, Sculpey, Cernit, Creal-Therm, and Fimo. Each of these is available in two-ounce or one-pound bars. The shelf life for the clays is generally two to five years, as long as they are kept at room temperature. Do not store your clay in areas over 80 degrees, as they will start to cure (get hard). Never put your uncured clay in the trunk of your car; this is a sure way to cure it prematurely. I mention this because it happens every summer in the warmer states. The question is always asked: "can I freeze the clay or keep it in an unheated room in the winter?" The answer is: yes, you may keep polymer clay in as cold an area as you like, it has no water in it so it won't freeze. It will become very firm, but as soon as you warm it up to room temperature, it is ready to sculpt.

Hundreds of rumors abound about how to cure polymer clay. The best way, and the only one I can recommend, is to follow the instructions on the label of the package in which the clay comes. The manufacturers have spent years developing the best way to cure their brand of clay. Most of the clays cure at 265-285 degrees in ten to fifteen minutes in a household oven.

Eyes

It is important to discuss the styles and types of eyes that do and don't work in making polymer dolls. Glass eyes are always the best because they withstand the temperatures required to cure a polymer doll without any problems at all. Porcelain eyes also withstand the temperatures, however, if they have a plastic coat over them to make them shine, the coating may be damaged if the temperature is higher than 280 degrees. Silicone eyes can withstand temperatures up to 300 degrees without any distortion or separation. Above that temperature, silicone eyes separate.

Acrylic eyes are generally not recommended, however, some of the acrylics of high quality hold their integrity up to temperatures of 300 degrees. If you choose to use acrylic eyes, I recommend testing them at 300 degrees before you spend hours making a polymer head only to find that the acrylic eyes melt while curing the doll head. You will know the eyes have failed if the iris and pupil separate from the white of the eye. If the heat becomes even hotter, the acrylic eyes melt and run down the face of the doll.

The style of eyes that I recommend is flat-backed glass eyes. The flat-backed eyes are easier to line up than the round or teardrop-style eyes. Generally, the finest eyes come from Germany, however, there are some very good glass eyes made in Asia that I also recommend. Generally, the difference between the glass eyes from Germany and those from Asia is the method of printing the iris. Those from Germany are hand painted; those from Asia are printed with a color printer. If you inspect the printed eyes closely, you will notice a

Glass Eyes

Silicone Eyes

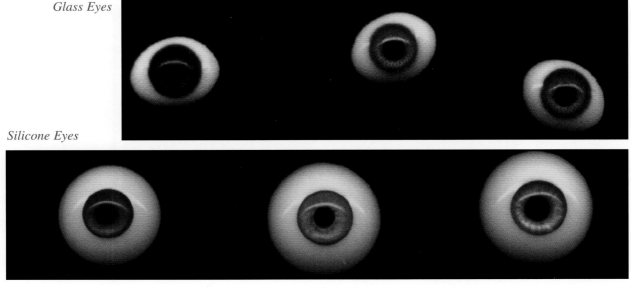

dot pattern in the printing process. Either of these types of eyes work just fine in polymer clay. The average person can tell the difference only through very close inspection.

Do not be fooled by eyes that include the word "glass" in their name. If any part of the eye is made of acrylic, it cannot withstand the temperatures required to cure the polymer dolls. Eyes that have acrylic in them cost less than half the price of glass eyes, but they melt. As with most dollmaking products; you get what you pay for. Quality always costs a little more, but the end product is worth the few extra dollars.

The only other thing that I would like to add about eyes is that they must have an ultra-violet protector in the color of the iris. Eyes that are made without an UV protector will eventually turn a sickening purple color after being exposed to sunlight. Today most glass, silicon or porcelain eyes of good quality will last indefinitely, keeping their beauty and color for centuries to come.

Hair

The hair recommended for polymer artdolls is natural hair from an animal that has been cleaned, dyed and prepared for the artist's use. With the exception of a few acrylic wigs of high quality, most synthetic hair is too thick and is the wrong scale for a doll. The best hair available is mohair from goats (alpaca or angora) or camel, llama, lamb and other fine wools. Hair of natural fiber is much more realistic for the scale and type of artdolls we show in this book.

The following photographs show the variety of mohair, from raw wool locks to the finest wefted and dyed alpaca. There are scores of different fibers available; not all come from those animals mentioned above. Hair fiber from other domestic and wild animals is also exciting and beautiful. The quality of the mohair you purchase generally depends on the price—again, you get what you pay for.

When considering hair and beards for your doll,

think about its style—ethnic origin, size and costuming. Many of the fibers available resemble hair on an African, Asian, American Indian, Hispanic, or a Caucasian person. Select your hair and bearding material when you are doing the initial planning for your creation. Remember that beard hair does not necessarily match head hair exactly. You may wish to mix a darker hue of the same type of hair for the beard.

Use actual hair samples, and hold them next to potential fabrics you are considering for the costuming. For example, if you have a print with a black background and a brown pattern selected for your costume you may wish to consider a brown tone for the hair. If you choose black, keep in mind that there may not be enough contrast to enhance the details of the costume. A cream-based fabric with a floral print may dictate that you use a cream-colored hair with a bit more yellow in

Various strands of fiber

Mohair curly fiber, natural salt-and-pepper and natural off-white

it to draw attention to the hair. If you are using silver as an accessory in jewelry you may wish to use gray hair for a great accent.

You can find a high quality of realistic fibers in many shades and colors. Colors ranging from dark to light are often available in the same fiber. Just as real human hair fades from sunlight, resulting in many shades and highlights, so, too, does animal hair. Merchants purchase fiber from vendors and ranchers all over the nation. Artists can purchase this mohair and other fibers from the sources listed on page 143.

You are dealing with luster, curl, texture, length and color, so choose your fibers with care. The breed and age of the animal results in different hair characteristics, as does the geographical origin of the fiber. Ranches all over the United States and the world have different environments, which produce differences in the animals' coats. Some regions develop different

crimps in the fiber from year to year; therefore you may like a breed from Southern California one year but hate it the next season. If you find a fiber you love, sample it with a few locks next to the costume you have chosen. Keep samples of the hair so you can try to match it closely when there is a new crop of fiber.

There are times when you cannot find the exact color of mohair you are looking for. Mohair goats grow primarily in white. Some farms raise gray, black or red, but these are rare. (Red is the rarest.) Sometimes you may have to dye the fiber to achieve a color you like. The easiest way to dye the fiber is to use Kool-Aid, Rit, Jaquard or Cushings dye products. Follow the directions on the product, and do not boil or agitate the fiber while you are dying it. The best method is to poke it down so it is submerged under the water, and then leave it to soak up the dye for the allotted time on the instructions. You may then spin the fiber in your washer and lay it out to

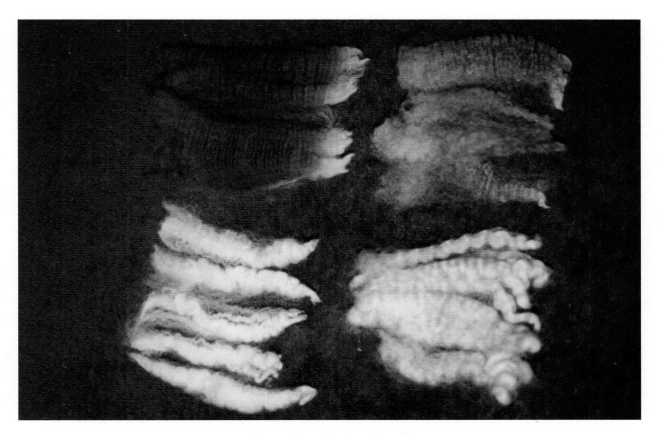

Four colors of crimped wool

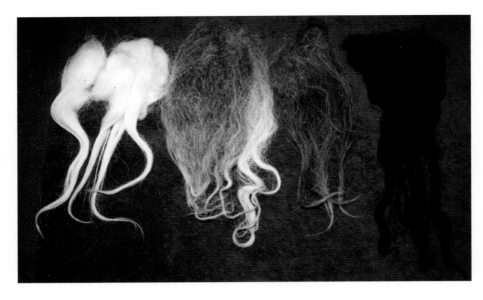

Fibers of four different colors.

dry on a towel in a well-ventilated area.

Mohair takes a bit more work than other fibers. It is highly regarded for its curl and luster, but it is so slick that it is hard to attach to the doll's head. I prefer to use wool when teaching beginning students, and mohair or alpaca for more advanced doll makers. Wool has a higher content of lanolin in it, which makes it easier to handle. Wool also has a much tighter crimp than mohair, which creates a more natural look on miniature dolls. You will quickly see which you like the best. Once you master one, you should try the others as you may find a new fiber that is just right for your dolls.

When the mohair is prepared for consumer use, the best is washed, tumbled and sewn into wefted strands for ease of applying to the doll head. Wefted mohair consists of locks of mohair that are sewn at one end into a long strand of hair. The manufacturer blunt cuts one end of the mohair and bends it over slightly, then sews a thin piece of paper in between the bent hair to hold it together. Wefted hair is generally sewn onto a skullcap in the process of making a wig. Other forms are open locks of hair; these strands of hair are generally used for applying hair directly to the head with glue.

Another method of preparing the wool or mohair is roving. Roving means combining all of the many small pieces of hair that are left over after the other processes take place into one long rope of hair. The wool or mohair is brushed and aligned to make sure that the fibers are in a long tube. One of the problems of using roving hair for your dolls is that the hair is left very short and without curl after the roving process. Some artists like the shorter, straight hair. Of course, because it is natural hair, you can bring it back to its curly body by spraying it lightly with water after it is placed on the doll. I like roving hair on an older doll like Mr. Claus or a pioneer woman. If you cut it very short and make a flocking length, it is also good for a man's "burr" hairstyle.

In the photos on the following pages, The Banjo Twins have cropped and crimped wool that fits their coloring perfectly. The Crow Warrior has long straight hair, which is natural for an American Indian. Santa Claus has long white wavy mohair. (This Santa was shown on the *Modern Masters* program on HGTV.) Nana has straight salt-and-pepper hair, which works well for an older woman wearing her hair up in a bun. The photo of The Teddy Bear Maker with short hair and a cropped beard also shows an elf with very long white mohair. The differences are extreme, but they work well together because of the character of each doll. (Thanks to Kris Crawford of Fireside Basics Dollhair for the technical information on fibers and the photos.)

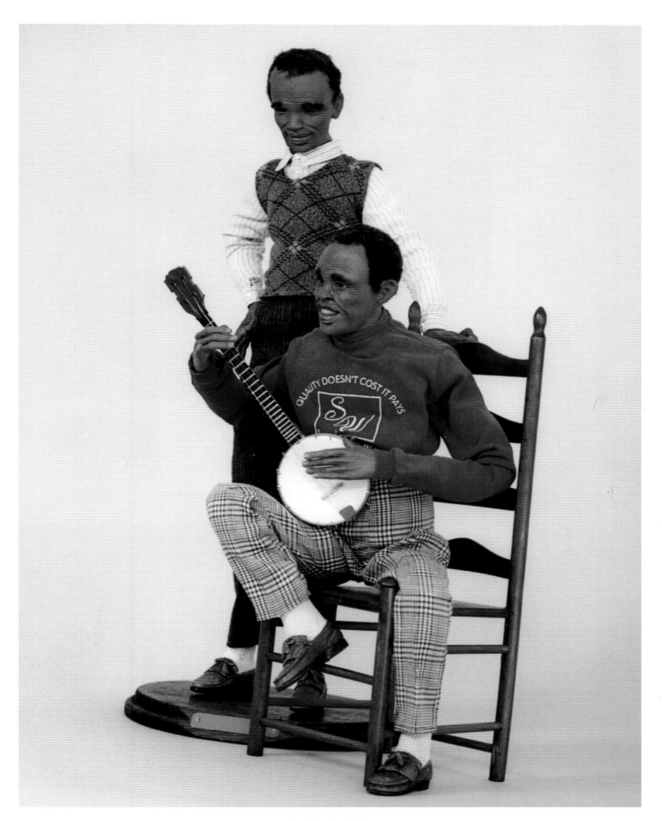

The Banjo Twins

Left: Crow Warrior
Below: Santa Claus
Bottom: Nana
Opposite page: The Teddy Bear Maker

CHAPTER 2
Anatomy

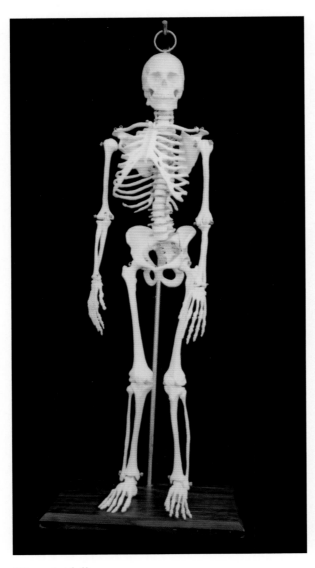

Understanding anatomy is as important to a sculptor as understanding the theory of music is to a composer. We spend our lives with other human beings, yet few of us truly understand our own anatomy. There is no better way to learn anatomy than by studying your own body and comparing your body parts with those in an anatomy book. I recommend using a pair of calipers (which can be found at any arts and crafts store) to measure your own body. You can then reduce the parts proportionately to the size of your sculpture. Any good anatomy book will give you great insight into the human anatomy, however, in most cases the books will not relate the length of one part to another. When sculpting a doll, for example, it is important to know how long the arm is in relationship to the head, the foot and other body parts. By measuring your own limbs, torso, hands, fingers and head you will find great similarities in dimension throughout the body. I think of these dimension similarities as "rules of thumb."

For example, I have a rule of thumb I call the "rule of the middle finger." One day, while sculpting a hand, I found that the inside middle finger was the same length as the width of the palm. I started measuring the rest of the body and found ten interesting similarities. The middle finger is also the same length as the palm from the bottom of the finger to the top of the carpal bones. It is the same as the height of the back of the hand from the carpal bones to the first knuckle of the middle finger. It is the same length as the distance from the hairline to the eyebrow, the eyebrow to the bottom of the nose and the bottom of the nose to the bottom of the chin. It is also the same width as one half of your face and the length of your ear. Interestingly enough, it is also the same as the width of your foot at the widest part. I call this phenomenon a rule, not a law, because it may vary slightly from person to person. Still, this rule is accurate enough to use in general sculpting.

There are other general rules measuring the anatomy that can be applied to sculpture, such as using the head as the base measurement. For example, the perfect adult body is eight heads tall, two heads wide and one head thick. The only person that is likely to be eight heads tall is a young athlete. The height of a person changes dramatically with age, of course. A newborn baby is only four heads tall, a five-year-old is five heads tall and a teenager is seven heads tall. An adult is seven and a half to eight heads tall, depending on gender and age. As we grow older, beginning in our late fifties, we start to shrink in height. By the time we are in our eighties, we may have shrunken as much as a full head in height. A 100-year-old person will have shrunk as

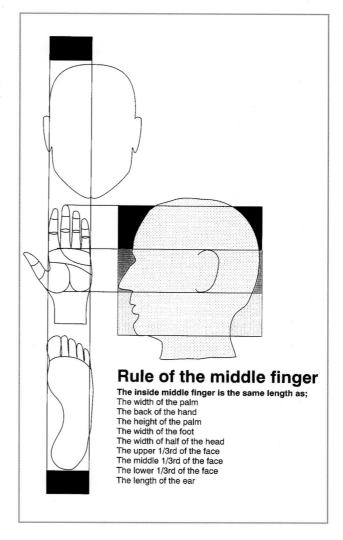

Rule of the middle finger
The inside middle finger is the same length as;
The width of the palm
The back of the hand
The height of the palm
The width of the foot
The width of half of the head
The upper 1/3rd of the face
The middle 1/3rd of the face
The lower 1/3rd of the face
The length of the ear

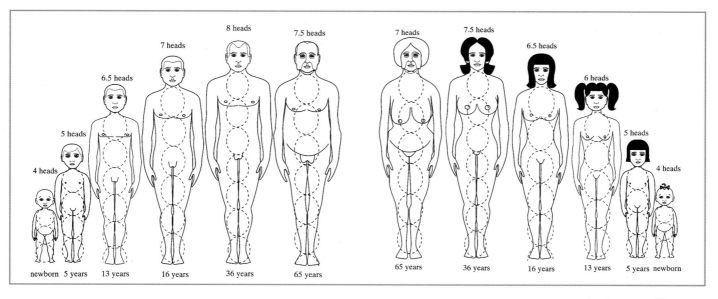

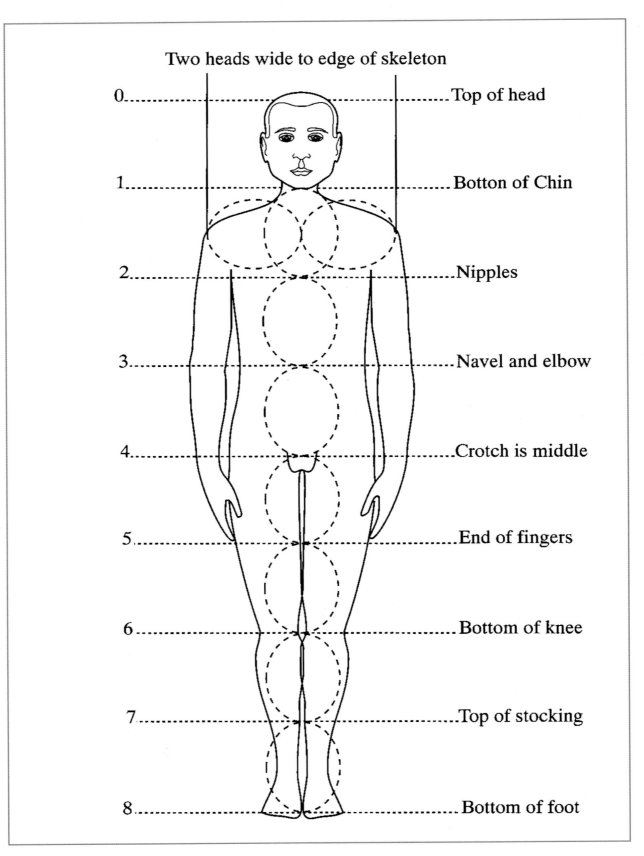

Two heads wide to edge of skeleton

0... Top of head

1... Botton of Chin

2... Nipples

3... Navel and elbow

4... Crotch is middle

5... End of fingers

6... Bottom of knee

7... Top of stocking

8... Bottom of foot

much as two heads in height due to curvature of the spine, loss of cushioning tissue between the vertebras and his or her over-all posture.

When sculpting a fashion doll it is common to exaggerate the height to ten heads tall. For example, Robert Tonner's fashion dolls are nine heads tall, as are Barbie, Gene and other fashion figures. Some even reach ten heads in height, yet look just right. Yet, when sculpting a Santa Claus it is acceptable to reduce the height of Santa to six heads. As we think of Santa as a "jolly old elf," it is okay to make him shorter and with a larger head.

It is not uncommon for famous artists to exaggerate the size of the human anatomy. For example, many sculptures by the renowned Italian artist Michelangelo's are ten heads tall, which creates a majestic appearance. On the other end of the height spectrum are the works of the famous French sculptor Rodin. His sculptures are often merely six heads high. Like Michelangelo, Rodin did this to make the human figure look stronger and more substantial. In both cases, the artists changed the anatomy to fit their own interpretation. They made the anatomy help tell the story they wanted to portray.

So it is okay to distort the height, width and even the relationship between the body and the head if it is done for a purpose, such as helping to tell the story of the figure you are sculpting. However, be sure that you have adjusted the size of the head/body for a reason and not just because you didn't know any better. The audience will know the difference.

Notice in the illustration on the opposite page that the perfect body is eight heads tall and two heads wide. The arms, torso and legs are also easily defined when measured against the size of the head. From the top of the head to the bottom of the chin is one head. The next measurement goes from the bottom of the chin to the nipple (two heads), then to the navel (three heads), to the bottom of the crotch (four heads), to the fingertips (five heads), to the knee (six heads), to the top of the stocking (seven heads) and finally to the bottom of the

foot (eight heads from top to bottom of the figure).

To further understand the anatomy for sculpting purposes, let's discuss the proportions of the head itself. The head is five eyes wide. We can measure the length of the head in thirds. From the hairline to the eyebrow is one third of the face; from the eyebrow to the bottom of the nose is another third of the face, and from the bottom of the nose to the bottom of the chin is the final third of the face.

The eyes and ears are both in the center third of the face. The tops of the ears are level with the top of the eyebrow, while the bottoms of the ears are level with the bottom of the nose. The distance from the eyebrow to the bottom of the chin is the same as the distance from the front tip of the nose to the front of the ear (forming a square).

The mouth is in the middle of the lower third of the face. The width of the mouth is even with the inside of the iris. A "hyper smile" occurs if you set the outside corner of the mouth in line with the outside of the iris.

On an adult, the head is the same height as the length of the foot. As an adult ages, the head gets smaller, as a result of the loss of fatty tissue and the grinding down of teeth. The jawbone also shrinks. Therefore, even though a human gets shorter with age, because the head has also grown smaller, he or she may still be eight heads tall.

There are also some interesting rules to follow with the hand. The length of the metacarpal bone is one and one half times the length of phalange (finger) number one, which is one and one half times longer than phalange number two, which is one and one half times longer than phalange number three. It may be easier to understand this if we move the other direction with this measurement, from the tip of the finger towards the back of the hand. The last bone of the finger is half the size of the middle bone of the finger, which is half the length of the largest bone of the finger, which is half the size of the metacarpal bone. This is a law of anatomy, not just a rule. It is the same on any healthy adult hand.

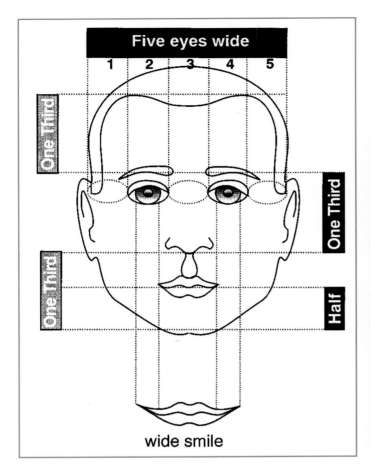

Five eyes wide

1 2 3 4 5

One Third

One Third

One Third

Half

wide smile

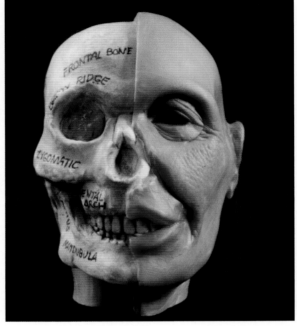

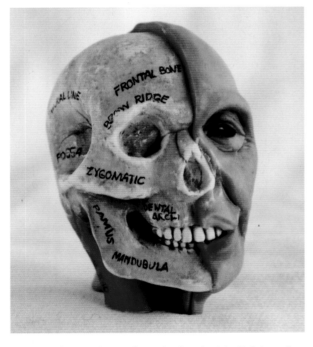

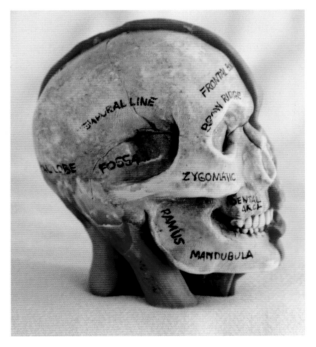

The photos above show the head with divisions for sculpting. In the photo above right, the clay over the head armature is 1/8-inch to 1/4-inch thich.

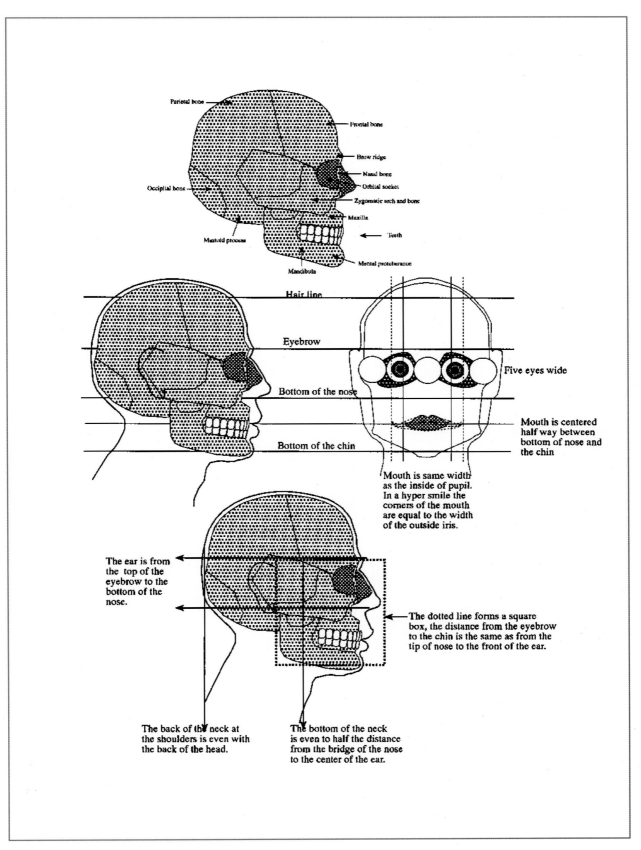

Parietal bone

Frontal bone

Brow ridge

Nasal bone

Orbital socket

Zygomatic arch and bone

Occipital bone

Maxilla

Teeth

Mastoid process

Mental protuberance

Mandibula

Hair line

Eyebrow

Five eyes wide

Bottom of the nose

Mouth is centered
half way between
bottom of nose and
the chin

Bottom of the chin

Mouth is same width
as the inside of pupil.
In a hyper smile the
corners of the mouth
are equal to the width
of the outside iris.

The ear is from
the top of the
eyebrow to the
bottom of the
nose.

The dotted line forms a square
box, the distance from the eyebrow
to the chin is the same as from the
tip of nose to the front of the ear.

The back of the neck at
the shoulders is even with
the back of the head.

The bottom of the neck
is even to half the distance
from the bridge of the nose
to the center of the ear.

The outside measurement of the fingers is 20 percent longer than the inside measurement of the same fingers. The reason for the discrepancy is the webbing of flesh between the fingers. Rather than try to measure the length of the webbing and scale it down to fit your sculpture, it is easier to know that the webbing between your fingers is found by laying a tool in the webbing and noticing it is at a 45-degree angle.

The hand can bend backward comfortably at a 45-degree angle. The word comfortable is very important. The hand will bend further, but it is not comfortable. If you make the doll look uncomfortable the consumers will not understand your sculpture, and will probably not purchase it. Always make the doll appear comfortable. The hand will also bend forward comfortably at a 45-degree angle and to the outside at a 45-degree angle. The hand will not bend inward comfortably, so don't force it, it will just look wrong.

It is very important to make the length of the arms and legs accurate when sculpting your doll. Nothing reveals amateurish sculpting faster than a doll with short arms and legs. If there is ever a question of how long to make the arms and legs, make them a little longer than you think they should be. When the doll is completed, clothed and posed the arms and legs will look foreshortened anyway. Remember that you can always shorten your doll, but it is nearly impossible to lengthen it.

I recommend memorizing the names of the bones of the head, arms, hands, legs and feet. The rest of the bones in the torso are not as important, although it wouldn't hurt to know them. Knowing the bones is very important to assuring that the sculpture is accurate in length and position.

Learning the clinical names of body parts will make it much easier to communicate with other sculptors. For example, rather than saying "I'm having trouble making that bump on the face," you could say, "I'm

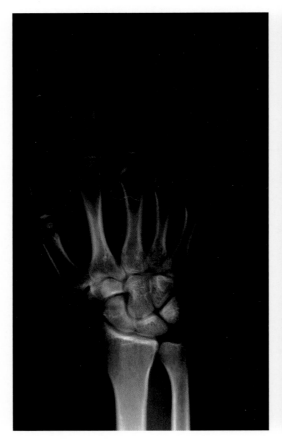 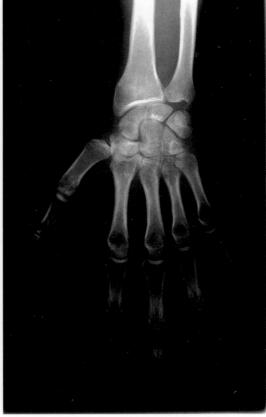

These x-ray photos show the bones of the right and left hands.

having trouble shaping the zygomatic arch." If you are this specific, anyone who understands anatomy will be able to help you.

Another example: it is very important to learn the parts of the ear. Notice in the illustration of the ear that each part has a name. Many artists sculpt the ear from memory and end up with something that looks more like a flower than a proper ear. If you take the time to memorize all of the parts of the ear by name and by recognition, you will be able to sculpt an ear that looks like an ear. The same holds true for the bones of the head and other parts of the body. A serious artdoll maker must know the anatomy, and even a hobbyist should know the basic bones and muscle groups.

Anatomy Books

The anatomy books that I recommend are those that are written for artists and not for the medical profession. Anatomy books written for the medical profession tend to be too detailed to be useful for the layman or artist. The books I recommend are those with illustrations of the anatomy and photographs that show gesture, as well as posing of the human figure. When choosing an anatomy book, look for those that indicate they are specifically aimed to help artists in sculpting or drawing the human figure. Two titles that I recommend are *Atlas of Human Anatomy for the Artist* by Stephen Roger Peck (Oxford Univeristy Press) and *Drawing the Head and Figure* by Jack Hamm (Perigee Books). These books can be found at most bookstores.

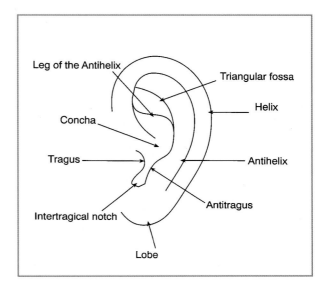

CHAPTER 3
Sculpting the Head

Inspiration for making dolls comes in many forms. Some artists are able to sculpt a figure directly from their imaginations. Others find inspiration in photographs or in people they see, whether they are strangers or familiar to them. I find the best method for me is a combination of the two: my imagination assisted by photos of many different characters. I may choose a mouth from one photo, eyes from another and a nose form still another. I like to combine different people's features as as to avoid the frustration of trying to sculpt a portrait. Once you have sculpted 20 or more dolls you may wish to try an exact portrait, but I don't recommend this for beginning dollmakers.

Some great sources for photos of interesting people are the older *National Geographic*, *Life* or *Saturday Evening Post* magazines. Any magazine that includes great photography can provide inspiration. Current publications are especially good for children and beautiful women.

Wherever you find your inspiration, once you begin your doll, sculpting the head is generally the first step. You can then use the head as the measuring point for the rest of the sculpture. It is easiest to get the eyes first and then make the doll to fit the eyes. As discussed in the chapter on anatomy, the head is five eyes wide, therefore five times the width of any eye equals the width of the face.

It is essential to use an armature under the clay when sculpting a polymer head. Using a Styrofoam egg as an armature is *not* recommended. Styrofoam melts in the oven and gives off toxic fumes. Other armatures, such as wooden eggs, metal, marble or even porcelain, expand with heat causing the polymer clay to crack during the curing process. I've tried many different armatures, but I have only found two that work consistently. The easiest to find is aluminum foil. Aluminum foil armatures have been used successfully for as long as artists have sculpted with polymer clay.

The newest, and one of the most exciting, breakthroughs in sculpting one-of-a-kind heads is the resin

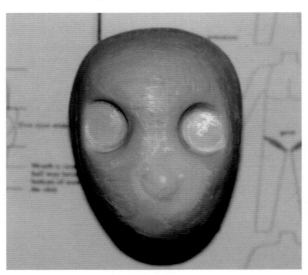

New resin head armature

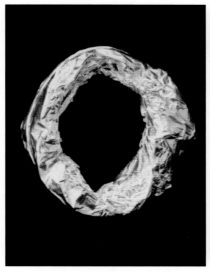

Aluminum foil ring in which to rest the head

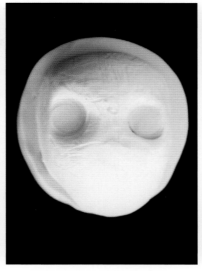

Head armature with clay on the back

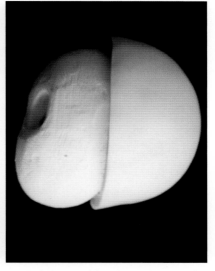

Side view of head armature with clay on the back

armature. Some years ago I designed a prototype armature and gave it to one of my students, Becky Alder. Becky made a two-part mold from the polymer sculpture and made a resin casting. After a few tries in sizing, thickness, and adding an air hole to avoid expansion, she began manufacturing resin heads. Both armatures are shown here; they work exactly the same. The resin saves time, and helps achieve a more accurate sculpt, but it does costs more, of course, than aluminum foil. (You can find it at Johnston Original Artdolls; see sources listing on page 143.)

Making an aluminum armature is simple in concept, but difficult in practical application. Follow the steps closely and then practice until you master the process. Use regular-weight aluminum foil. Cut a length of foil about two feet long. Begin crinkling the foil at one end. Keep crinkling it together until you have a ball about three inches high. Continue to compress the ball into the finished shape of a human skull about two-and-a-half inches high. This completed armature will serve to make a head for an 18- to 20-inch doll. Depending on the amount of clay you use to cover the armature, you may expand this armature to make a head three to three-and-a-half inches high.

Now smooth the surface of the foil with a wooden dowel or the backside of a spoon. I use a dowel that is four inches long and half an inch in diameter to smooth the aluminum foil. I also use the dowel to press imprints into the foil for the eye sockets. If you are making an adult, the eyes should be in the middle one third of the head; if you are making a child, the eyes and brow bone are just below the half way point of the height of the head. This placement create a very high forehead for the child.

You are now ready to sculpt the head. From this point on, the process is the same whether you have used an aluminum foil head armature or a resin head armature. Prepare a ball of clay about the size of a small plum; flatten it into a pancake one-quarter-of-an inch thick. Place the pancake on the back of the head as shown in the photographs. Be sure that the clay is no thicker than one-quarter of an inch, and that it is completely smooth. You may smooth the clay with the palm of your hand or with your fingers. Cut the excess clay from the leading edge of the skullcap, thus preparing the "half skull" for the oven. Before placing the armature in the oven, make a small donut-shaped frame of aluminum foil for the head to rest in. It should be just large enough for the armature to rest in, so that it won't roll over in the oven. Place the head face down in the aluminum frame, not allowing any of the wet polymer clay to touch the aluminum. Put the frame and the armature in the oven at 275º for ten minutes.

The times and temperatures specified in this book are standard for most polymer clays, but are specific for ProSculpt©. The same process may be used for all polymer clays; however, the time and temperature will vary slightly. Whichever clay you use, you will find the correct time and temperature indicated on the accompanying instructions.

Eyes

Upon completion of the baking cycle, allow the head to cool completely before continuing the sculpt (approximately ten minutes). Once the half skull has cooled, you may proceed by placing eyes in the sockets. Glass, porcelain, and silicon eyes accept oven temperatures up to and including 300 degrees. Therefore, these are the only eyes I recommend to be used in polymer dolls. As polymer does not deteriorate with time, these dolls will likely be around for hundreds of years, so use the best eyes you can afford. There are only two cautions when choosing eyes; first, ask if the eyes have an UV protective coating to keep them from turning color in the sun. Second, be sure that the eyes are flat backed, which makes it easier to mount them to the armature.

Place the eyes in the sockets and put a worm-shaped piece of polymer clay around each eye to hold it in place. Smooth the clay until it conforms to the armature. Once again, place the half skull in its aluminum frame, face up this time, and place it in the oven for ten minutes at 275 degrees.

While the head is cooling, make another pancake the same size as the first. After the head has cooled, apply the pancake to the front of the armature by butting the faceplate up to the edge of the back half of the cured section. Form the clay to fit firmly against the armature; be sure no air is trapped beneath the clay. Take care to remember where the eyes are when you

seal the new clay down to the armature. With the clay covering the entire face, press the clay toward the eyes to create eye sockets and to expose the eyes. Once you see the eyes through a thin layer of clay, stop pressing. Cut a slit through the soft clay from one side of the eye horizontally to the other side over the top of the eyes, forming a sleeping eye. Open the eye with your primary sculpting tool by pressing up on the upper lid and down on the lower lid. You are only beginning the process; so don't try to make beautiful eyes just yet.

Nose

Once the eyes are open, place a ball of clay half the size of the ball you made for the faceplate on the bottom of the head armature at the location of the chin. Shape this clay into the mandible, or jawbone. Smoothing the mandible to the existing clay can be accomplished with your thumb, tools and the palm of your hand. Next, using your thumb and first finger, pinch a nose out of the existing clay.

The nose should be smaller than you expect the finished nose to be, as it will expand during the sculpting process, when you put in the nostrils. Once you have the basic shape of the nose sculpted, place your sculpting tool in one nostril at a time, and spin the tool around until you are pleased with the shape and size of the nostril.

Mouth

Moving down the face half way between the bottom of the nose and the base of the chin, score a line representing the mouth. This line should be one quarter-of-an-inch deep, so as to allow you to manipulate the upper lip up and the lower lip down. I use the flat side of the primary sculpting tool to form the lip. Tucking the top lip down into the scored line and tucking the bottom lip up into the same spot forms the corners of the mouth. By rolling and tucking the lips inward, you will form a human lip. (The corner of the mouth is formed by the obicularus oris muscle, which goes

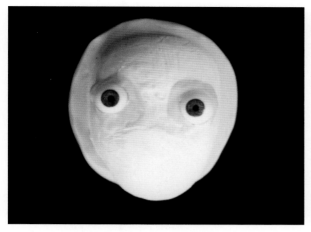

Faceplate sculpted head with eyes open

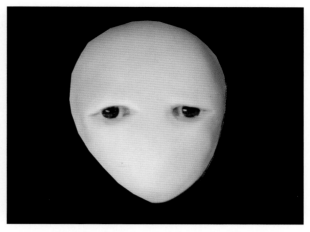

Half head sculpted with eyes in place

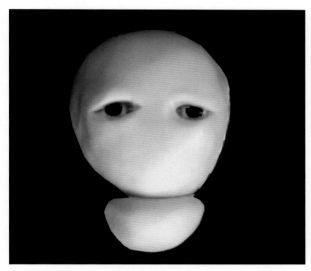

Faceplate sculpted head with additional clay on chin

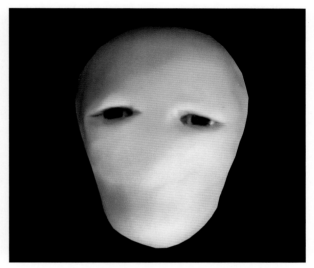

Faceplate sculpted with clay on chin smoothed into the face

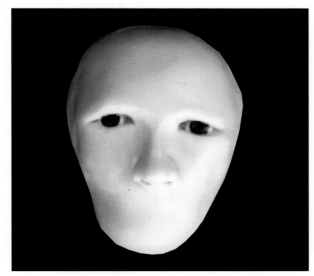

The nose rough sculpted on to the faceplate

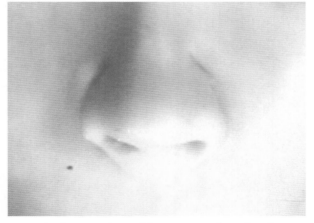

A close-up view of the nose rough sculpted on to the faceplate

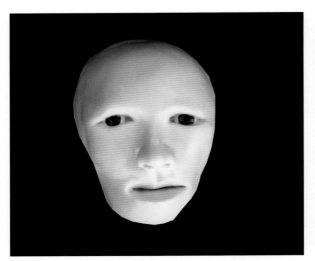

The beginnings of the mouth's formation

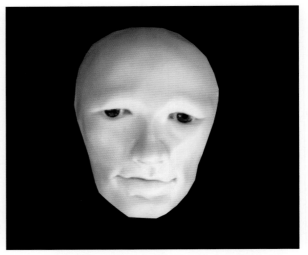

The mouth formed with obicularus showing in the corners of the mouth

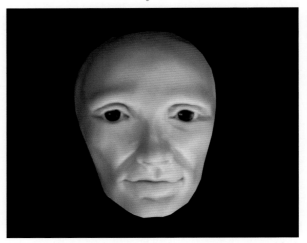

The finished face before the character lines are added

around the entire mouth, and attaches to the triangularis muscle. The obicularus oris muscle helps you pucker up for a kiss or form a pursing shape with your lips. It is evident as a small mound in the corners of the mouth).

After forming the upper and lower lip, put in the filtrum, which is the indentation in the center of the upper lip, just below the nose. The fullness of the lips will be determined by the thickness of the faceplate. If the lips are too thin, you may add more clay by making a worm-like roll of clay and placing it on the top and bottom edge of the lips. If the lips are too thick, you may remove a little clay from the lips with the edge of your primary sculpting tool or a craft knife.

Eyebrows and Eyelids

Form the brow ridge by pressing down with your thumb above the eye until a ridge is formed. Do the same to form the cheekbone; press up on the fat below the eyes to form the zygomatic arch (cheekbone). This process is best understood by looking at the photo above right, which shows the mounds for the cheeks and eyebrows.

Form the upper and lower eyelids by pressing into the clay above the eyes and then smoothing the clay until the lid is evident. The lower lid is formed by pressing your sculpting tool into the clay from the inside cor-

ner of the eye outward to the outside corner. This is a pressing method, not a cut into the clay.

Refining the Face

Now that you have formed the brow, eyes, nose, lips, cheekbones, jaw bones and chin, you are ready to put in identifying character features. First, check to see if the eyes have peripheral vision. Look at the head from the side, checking to see the white or sclera of the eye. If you can't see the white, pull the clay back on the sides of the eye. Note that once you have pulled the clay back, you will have to remove it from the face to make the side of the face look thin enough. I press the clay

The open mouth without teeth

The open mouth with teeth on top and bottom

toward the back of the head until it comes off near the joining line of the back of the head. The series of photos shows each step in the turn in which it is completed.

The next step is to open the mouth and put in the teeth. Open the mouth by inserting your sculpting tool between the lips. Press the lower lip down. The upper lip stays in place just as it does on a human when he or she opens their mouth. Lower the lip until you have room to put in the tongue and teeth. Form the tongue by pressing a scoring line into the existing clay in the mouth until the tongue is shaped. Make the teeth by creating a small ball of translucent clay and then forming it into a horseshoe-shaped bridge. Put the bridge in the top of the mouth, and attach it to the upper roof of the mouth. Make another bridge and attach it in front of the tongue to the gum between the lower lip and the tongue. Refer to the photo above right to understand where it goes. With both the upper and the lower bridge in place, use a scalpel to cut lines between the central incisors, lateral incisors, k-9, and bicuspids. The scalpel is very thin and adds to the realism of the spaces between the teeth. Smooth the edges of the teeth with your primary sculpting tool. Make the lateral incisors a little shorter than the central incisors. This makes the doll appear a little younger. The older we get the more we grind down our teeth, so if you want to make a very old per-

son, smooth the teeth on the bottom until they appear to be ground down with use. With age they become flat across the bottom.

To age the eyes, make a sagging lower lid with wrinkles. Scoring (making gentle lines in the clay) the tool into the clay makes the basic shape for the wrinkles. Round the scored lines to look like skin folds. Always score in the wrinkles, rather than cutting them into the clay, to assure that the lines look natural. If you aren't sure where the wrinkles go, use your own face as a model, or the face of a family member who is willing to help. The wrinkles at the outer corner of the eyes are called crow's feet because they resemble the three toes of a crow's foot. When studying these wrinkles closely, you will detect that there are more than three wrinkles. Because of the dynamics of the fold, however, they come in sets of three. Therefore, if you wish to have more than three there will be six, nine, twelve or more, but always a multiple of three. I recommend you put in all of the wrinkles you see while looking into the mirror, thus assuring realism. If you don't have wrinkles, ask an older member of your family to pose for you, or use a photo. If you are sculpting a child, you obviously don't need to concern yourself with wrinkles.

The lines extending from the side of the nose to the side of the mouth are called the extension of the nasal furrow. The lines extending from the corners of the mouth are called the extensions of the obicularus. They extend down from the corner of the mouth to the middle of the chin. On a very old and heavy person, they may even go under the chin to help form a double chin.

As we age, our faces start to sag. We can illustrate this by pushing down on the jowls until they seem to hang at the base of the jaw. The eyebrows may be pushed down on the outside edges to show a tired look. Pressing up on the inside corner of the eyebrows creates a passive, yet happy, expression.

Pressing up on the outside corner of the mouth creates a nice smile. Remember, if the person is in a "hyper smile" the outside edges of the mouth line up with the outside edge of the eye's iris. Pulling down on the tip of the nose adds years to the face without a great deal of work. The best way to age the face is to push up on the chin, which makes the distance from the bottom of the chin to the bottom of the nose smaller and makes the face look as though it has lost its teeth. The harder you push up on the chin, the older your character will appear. Notice in the photos that I have changed a young man to a very old one by making a few wrinkles, sagging the jowls and pressing the chin up toward the nose.

Once all of the wrinkles are in place and the face is nearly finished, apply the texture from the horsehair brush. Press the brush into the clay over the top of the deeper wrinkles you have already sculpted. Press the horsehair brush into the soft clay in two directions: first, put the brush in at a 45-degree angle, then turn it 90 degrees and press it into the soft clay again. I lay the brush into the skin several times until I like the effect it is creating.

Once all of the features are in, use a small firm brush to smooth the clay around the eyes, mouth and nose. By applying a small amount of smoothing oil to the brush you will be able to remove all of the tool marks.

Now you're ready to put the face in the oven. Set the face upright in the aluminum frame so no part of the soft clay is touching the ring or any part of the oven. Cure the face for ten minutes at 275 degrees. When the face has cured and cooled, remove the face from the oven and go on to the next step: sculpting the neck.

Neck

To make the neck, start with a ball of clay about the size of a small plum. Roll the plum-sized ball into the shape of a tootsie roll, and then flatten the roll into a rectangular shape. Cut the ends off of the rectangle to make two straight edges. Now, roll the two ends of the rectangle together and seam them into one shape, much like a napkin ring. Cut a notch in the end of the cylinder to create a space for the chin to fit in. Refer to the photo below to better understand the shape of the neck with the notch cut in it.

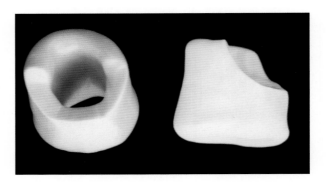

The neck is shown in a cylinder shape and from the side.

Seam the cylinder to the head to complete the basic neck. Shape it until you like the look. If you wish to age the neck, sculpt in "turkey flesh" wrinkles by pinching the clay with your thumb and first finger. Put in additional wrinkles to fit the age of the character you are working on.

The muscle running from behind the ear to the tip of the clavicle bone (also known as the collarbone) is called the sternomastoid clavicle process. This muscle, which is seen most clearly on very thin or muscular people, is important to complete the shape of the neck. Making a small roll of clay and laying it on the head

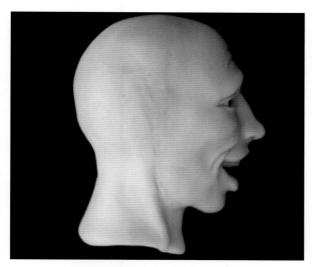

Sculpted head with neck attached

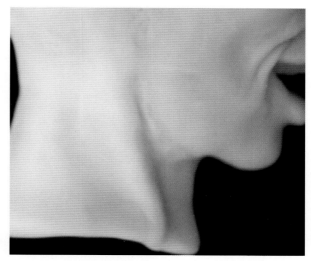

Sternomastoid clavicle process in place

from behind the ear to the tip of the clavicle will form the muscle. Now shape it with your fingers and tools until it looks like the photo above.

Ears

Once the neck is finished, you are ready for the ears. Sculpting the ears can be very challenging, or it can be done simply if you follow the outlines in the diagram at right. I recommend sculpting the ears one at a time and curing the first one before sculpting the second, as we have a tendency to smash one ear while we are making the other if it isn't cured first. Make the ear by rolling a small ball out of clay. The ball should be the size of a small pea. Flatten the pea until it is no larger than a dime. Place the ear on the side of the head. The hole of the ear should be exactly in the middle of the head from top to bottom and from front to back. You may draw an imaginary line from the eyebrow to the top of the ear and from the bottom of the nose to the bottom of the ear to find the right spot. The distance of the ear from the nose is the same as from the eyebrow to the bottom of the chin. If you drawa line from the eyebrow to the chin and one from the tip of the nose to the front of the ear, this should help you place the ear where it belongs.

Smooth the ear into the basic outline shape of an ear

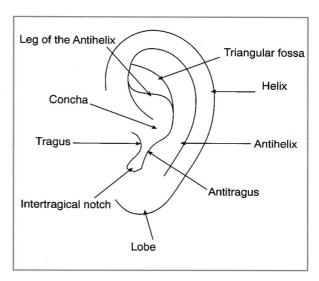

by cutting away excess pieces of clay and by pressing the clay down firmly against the head. Press a "C" into the ear with the ear tools as shown in the illustration. This indentation—the curved rim of the outer ear—is called the helix. Then press the tool deep into the ear to make the conch-shaped part of the ear. Next, pull down on the bottom of the ear to form the earlobe. Just in front of the earlobe is the tragus; it is formed by pressing a small lobe of clay inward toward the conch. Just under the ring of the helix, press in the triangular fossa and the legs of the anti helix. Follow the illustration and photographs to see that all of the parts of the ear are in place. Once all of the elements are in the ear, smooth each part with your ear tool and a firm brush. The last thing is to gently push forward on the anti helix. Smooth out the unwanted tool marks by adding a small amount of diluent or smoothing oil to the end of your brush.

Put the head in the oven to cure the neck and the first ear. It is best to put the head on the aluminum curing ring upside down. Put the hardened top of the head in the ring. Do not allow any of the aluminum curing ring to touch any of the finely sculpted features of the face as it can distort them.

Make the second ear just as you did the first. Cure it in the oven, again making sure that none of the finished face is touching any part of the metal in the oven or of the aluminum curing ring.

Hat

When the head is finished, you may choose to make a hat. One of the only ways to get a hat that fits your sculpture perfectly is to sculpt it right onto the head. I use raw clay to make the hat. Just put a ball of clay on the head and start pressing it into shape. You can be as creative as you like. Once the hat is finished cure the head again at the same temperature and time. Paint the hat with acrylic paint. I recommend painting a thin wash of color over the hat and once it has dried, paint a second coat to make the color richer. I often use as many as four coats of paint to get the exact color I like. Painting in these washes helps to put depth in your paint. Since the hat is sculpted right on the head and cured to the head, it will stay there indefinitely. When making a hat of clay on the head, do not put hair on first. You may put hair on the head around the base of the hat after the hat is cured.

Hair

Before applying the mohair to the head it's a good idea to construct a headstand to hold the head. Cut a block of wood four inches by four inches by one inch thick. Drill a one-eighth-inch hole in the center of the block of wood and insert a one-eighth-inch dowel about six

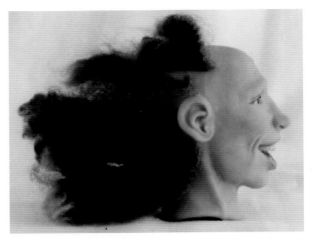

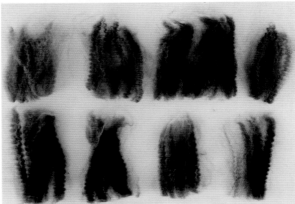

Top: A side view of the head offers a good look at the completed ear. Above: Place 16 small locks of mohair into separate piles.

inches long into the hole. Glue the dowel into the hole to make it secure. Place the finished head on the dowel as a resting-place while you apply the hair and complete the hairstyle. The headstand also serves as a place to keep the head while you move on to the next step in making the doll. The one pictured is made of resin with a brass tube for the head to rest on. It is one that I use for showing display heads.

Mohair wigs are the most realistic of all the doll wigs. Making the mohair fit directly to the head without a wig or scull cap is even more realistic. Choose the mohair you wish to use (see pages 16-18 for guidance on choosing mohair) and separate 16 small locks into piles as shown in the photo above.

Spread the lock of hair about one-and-a-half inch-

These photos illustrate the step-by-step process of putting on the mohair.

es wide. Apply a thin strip of Fabri-Tac Glue (which may be purchased at any local craft store) on the back of the head, from the bottom of one ear to the bottom of the other ear. While the glue is wet, lay one of the locks in the glue and press it down firmly until it is well into the glue. Do not put so much glue on that it comes through the hair or presses out to the side. Allow the first line of glue to set for a few minutes. Put another line of glue one-half inch above the first line and apply a lock of hair in the same process. Continue laying on locks of hair until you have completed four lines up the back. Now, lay one lock of hair running vertically at the front of the ear. This lock will represent the leading edge of the hairline. If you are making

a male, point the hair roots forward as though the hair is growing out of the skin on the side of the head. If you are making a female, point the roots toward the back of the head, with the feathered end coming toward the face. This will allow you to style the hair into a male or female hairstyle. Note that the hair on a human's head grows away from the crown; therefore place the hair on your doll just as it grows on a human.

Continue laying locks around the crown. The hair in front of the crown should be lying with the roots toward the crown and the long end of the locks lying toward the face. Again, this will facilitate combing the hair into a style that fits the doll.

Even though the glue will be dry to the touch in

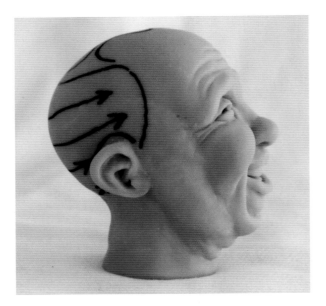

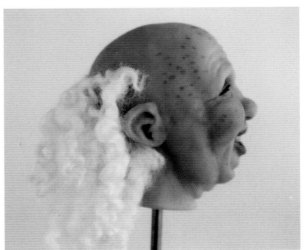

Top photos: Rings drawn on the head show where to place the hair.

Above photos and opposite page: Choice of hair placement on the head and face changes the character.

less than ten minutes, it should sit overnight for a firm hold. Once the glue is set, comb out the hair. Use a single needle as your comb. Hold the hair at the base and comb through the long hair to work out any kinks or knots. Once you have combed through each lock, you may comb the locks together. Be careful not to pull out too much hair out during the combing process. If there are bare spots, fill them with glue and additional locks of hair. Or, if you like, you may also fill any small bare areas with flocking from the hair left over from the application of hair. Cut the remaining hair into tiny bits

that are only a fraction of an inch long each. Put glue into the bare areas between the locks and then press the flocking into those areas. It will cover all of the bare spots and make the finished hairstyle blend better into the skull more realistically.

Side burns, eyebrows and even a short-cropped beard may be applied the same way. This short stubble beard may also be used as a short hairstyle with a very realistic effect. The hair will be extremely wild and frightening when you first apply it to the head. Give the glue a chance to harden properly and then style the

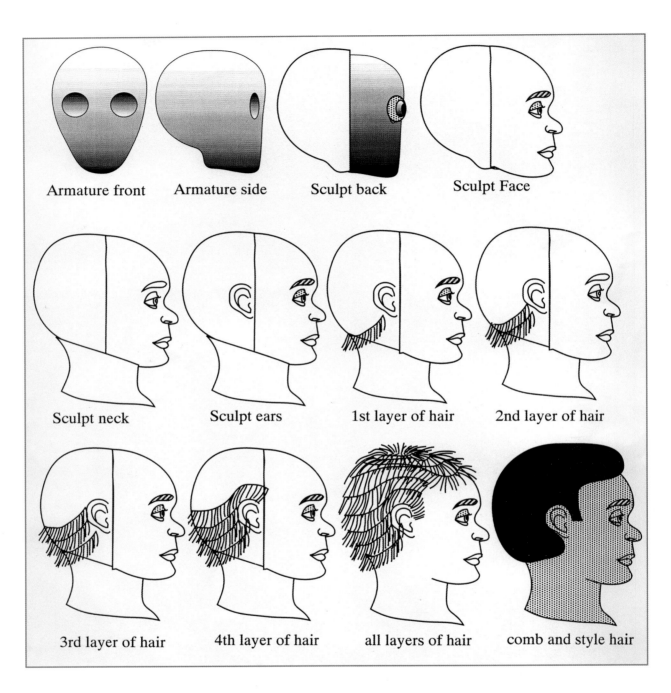

Armature front   Armature side   Sculpt back   Sculpt Face

Sculpt neck   Sculpt ears   1st layer of hair   2nd layer of hair

3rd layer of hair   4th layer of hair   all layers of hair   comb and style hair

hair the way you want it. You may style the hair much as you would on a human head. As the hair is natural, you may moisten it and roll in up on rollers made from straws of various sizes. Let the hair dry over night, and then comb it out and style it to your liking. If you wish to restore the integrity of the natural wave or curl all you need to do is lightly spray the hair with water; it will kink up just like human hair.

When applying a beard, put a line of glue from the bottom of the ear under the chin to the bottom of the other ear. Apply a lock of hair from the bottom of the ear to the bottom of the chin. Now apply another from the chin to the other ear. Apply a line of glue from the side burn down towards the jaw, and then in a curving

The Teddy Bear Maker has short hair and cropped beard; the elf has a long white mohair beard and hair.

fashion up to the corner of the mouth. The last lock of hair should be laid vertically on the upper lip and down the side of the mouth until it touches the other locks of hair. Notice in the photographs that the hair on the face generally grows down. Once the mustache is finished, and has dried overnight, cut the excess hair at the bottom of the upper lip to shape the mustache. Leave some long hair on the sides of the upper lip to blend into the rest of the beard. Refer to the close-up photo of the mustache and the completed hairstyle at right for help in understanding this process.

If you wish to make a short-cropped beard, cut very short hair into a pile of flocking. Put glue on the head everywhere you wish the hair to stick. Put the flocked hair into the glue and pat it down with your fingers. Do not let the glue come through the hair; it will turn shiny and even white when it dries. Once the glue is set, give the doll a haircut and trim around the edges. If you have a few bare spots, just add glue in the bare spots and apply more flocked hair.

This character features a short-cropped beard

CHAPTER 4
Sculpting the Hands

Hands are made after the head is completed. The process of making the doll must always start with the head; this allows you to size the hand and the rest of the body parts in proportion to the head.

Using a hand armature to make the hands is the easiest and most accurate way to assure that your hands are correct. I recommend purchasing pre-made hand armatures; these are not expensive and will save you a great deal of time and trouble trying to find all of the materials used for making the armature. (See Sources listing on page 143.)

If you decide to make your own hand armatures you will need a roll of 16-gauge copper wire, a brass tube 3/16ths of an inch in circumference, a roll of alu-

minum plumber's tape and a roll of floral tape. Cut ten copper wires two-and-a-half inches long for the fingers, and put five of them in the brass tube to represent fingers. Crimp the brass tube with the fingers in it to lock them in place. Spread the fingers apart in the shape of a hand and then apply a piece of aluminum tape (one-and-a-half inches long by one-half-inch wide) over the base of the four fingers, to hold them together. The photos on page 45 will help you understand where to put the aluminum tape.

Using a strand of paper tape 15 inches long, wrap the tape around the brass tube from the bottom toward the palm. Stretch the tape and wrap it around the arm base, the wrist and the palm. Wrap the tape up the first

 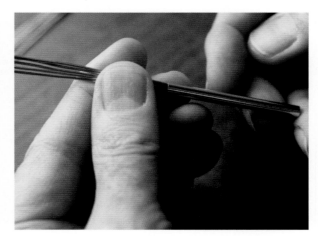

Cut copper wires to form the finger armatures. Slide the armatures half way into the brass tube and then crimp the tube to hold them in.

The aluminum tape forms the armature for the palm.

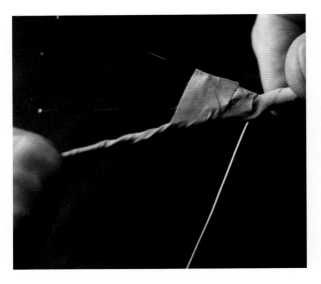

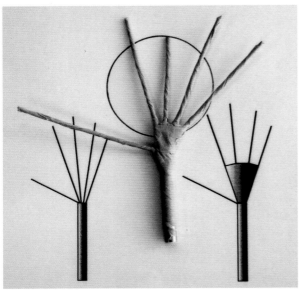

*Top photos: Wrap the wires and brass tube snugly with paper tape to create the covering for the hand armature.
Above: Use a circular template to help cut the fingers to the right length.*

finger to the end of the finger and then break it off. Wrap each finger by wrapping around the palm first and then up each individual finger. When all five fingers are wrapped, twist the paper on each finger tightly so that the paper is snug against the fingers. This helps ensure that the clay sticks to the armature.

Place the hand armature on the face of the doll, with the base of the hand placed on the chin and the middle finger lying across the brow bone. Cut the middle finger off at the brow line to make it the right length for the hand armature. Remember this is a hand armature you are making, so don't be alarmed that it looks too short for the finished hand. The clay will extend beyond the finger armatures to make it the proper length for the correct anatomy.

With the middle finger cut to length, make a template to assist in cutting the other fingers and thumb. Draw a circle two inches in diameter. Lay the tip of the middle finger at the top of the circle. With all five fingers pointing upwards, an equal distance apart

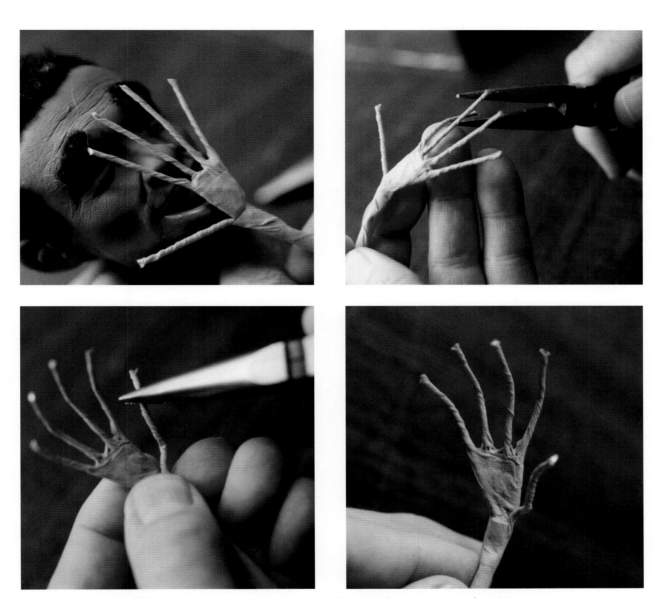

When the fingers are the proper length, curve them into natural positions.

from one another, mark each finger with a pencil where it crosses the rounding line of the circle. The illustration on the opposite page will help you understand this process.

Once you have marked each of the fingers, cut them off at the pencil line, spread them apart and look at them. Are you satisfied with their length? If not, cut them again until the hand looks accurate as an armature. You may wish to hold up your own hand and look at the length of your fingers in relationship to each other and to the armature you have just made. The armature should be a miniature replica of your own hand.

Bend the wrist of your armature in the direction you wish to make the finished hand. To indicate a passive gesture, the wrist should be bent forward, almost as though it is hanging limp. To indicate an active gesture, bend the wrist backward.

Now bend a radial into the palm so the fingers have a natural curvature. The radial is the curved part of the hand that extends from the index finger to the lit-

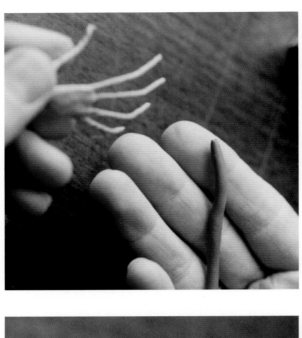
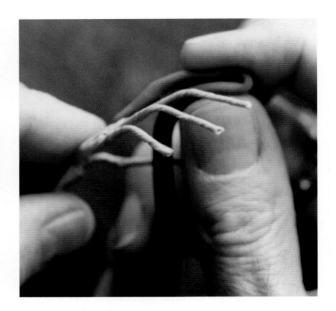
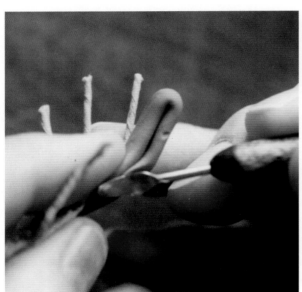

Once the fingers are natually curved, apply clay to each one.

tle finger. The radial should be curved toward the palm. Bend the first knuckle of each finger down slightly. Bend the second knuckle of each finger slightly down to make a very natural-looking pose. Do not bend the third knuckle, as it will have a tendency to look too much like a claw. We will put a third knuckle in with clay, but not with a metal armature.

Bending the thumb into an "L" shape forms the thumb. Hold the thumb at the base and bend it up toward the other fingers. Place the pliers halfway up the thumb and bend the tip of the thumb out in an "S" shape. If you hold your hand up and look at your own thumb, you will better understand the shape you need to achieve.

Make a thin roll of clay, shaped like a worm and twice the length of each finger. Put one strip of clay over the first finger, starting at the base and working it over the top of the finger and down the other side.

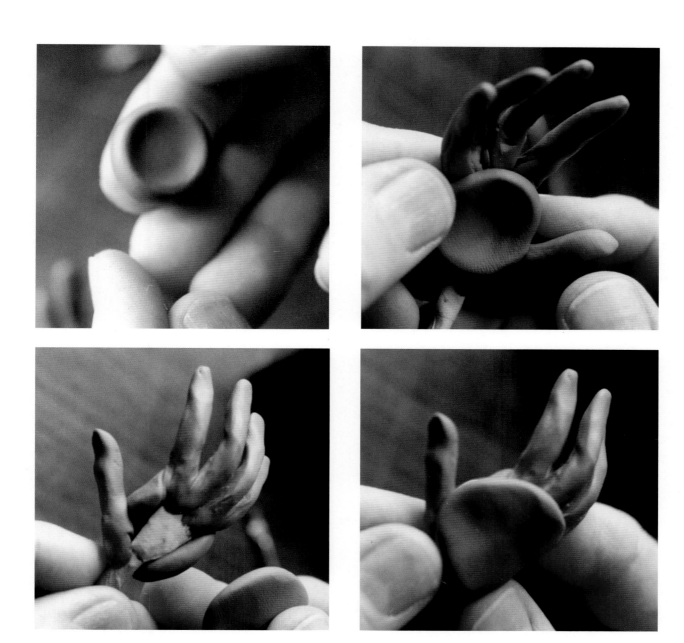

To create the palm and back of the hand, apply a flattened piece of clay to each side of the armature.

Smooth the seams on either side of the finger until the finger is solidly placed on the armature. Repeat this process with each of the five fingers.

Shape a piece of clay into a ball about the size of a small grape. Flatten the middle of the ball until it looks like a jelly doughnut. This will form the palm of the hand. Lay the piece of clay at the base of the knuckles of the fingers and against the inside of the thumb.

Attach a hemostat to the hand armature by putting one tongue of the hemostat up the tube at the base of the armature and locking it. The purpose of the hemostat is to hold the hand armature while you are working on it. It also gives you something to hold the finished hand in the oven while it cures.

Make a ball the size of a plum. Roll the ball into a cylinder shape (like a tootsie roll) about 1½ inches long. Cut the cylinder in half, as a hot dog bun is cut. Place the cylinder on the armature to serve as the fore-

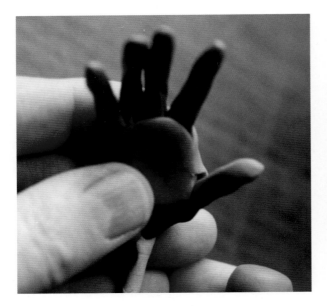

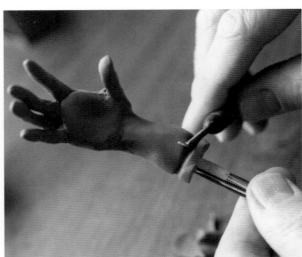

Create the wrist and forearm by applying a hot-dog-bun-shaped piece of clay.

arm and wrist. Smooth all of the parts together to make the basic shape of the hand and arm.

Smooth the wrist to the hand and then shape the arm and wrist to resemble a human likeness. Cut the excess clay from the bottom of the wrist up to the brass tube. Put a ring called a stitch button of clay around the base of the arm. This ring provides a place to attach the body stocking later after you cure the hand in the oven.

Next, form the knuckles on each finger. Look closely at the photograph. Notice there is a curved scoring line on the knuckle. Put in another curve, fac-

ing the opposite direction, and a straight line in the center of the two curves.

Turn the hand over and expose the palm in preparation for sculpting the under side of the hand. Score half moon curved lines at the base of each finger, two lines in the middle of each finger and one curve at the last knuckle. These should resemble skin folds at the three joints. Build up the pad of flesh around the palm of the hand until the muscles look correct. The muscle at the base of the thumb is called the thenar; the muscle opposed to the thenar is called the hypothenar.

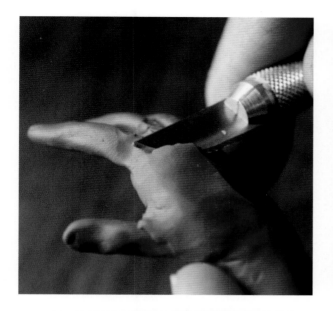

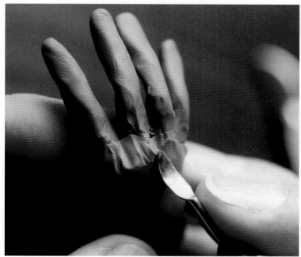

After smoothing the clay on the back of the hand, create the fingernails with the primary sculpting tool.

These two together are often called the heel of the hand. You can easily find these on your own hand if you look at your palm and pinch your thumb and little finger together. The two muscles that protrude are the thenar, at the base of your thumb, and the hypothenar at the base of your little finger. Both of the muscles need to be added to make the palm of the hand look realistic. Form the lines on the palm by looking at the ones on your own hand. You may form as many lines as you may like in the hands to make them realistic.

The fingernails are formed by pressing the finger-nail portion of the 3-1 tool into the uncured clay at the tip of each finger. Press the tool into the clay and make an imprint, much like making a mold impression at the tip of each finger. Once there is a basic imprint of a fingernail on each finger, make a small translucent white fingernail to place on each nail bed. Make a tiny ball of translucent clay for each fingernail. Flatten the ball into an artificial fingernail between your own first finger and thumb. Place the new nail on the fingernail bed, seal it down and shape it with the primary sculpting tool. Form the cuticles with your sculpting tool.

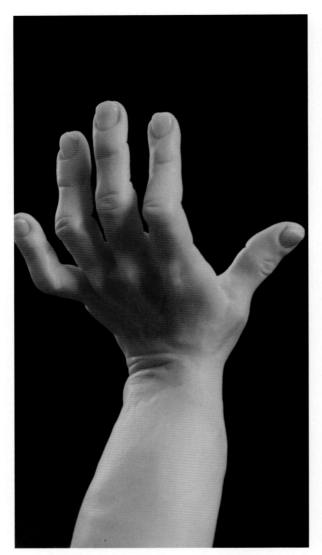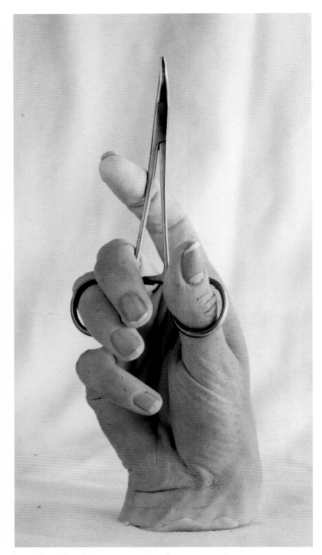

The final touches on the hand include painting the nails and adding paint or a wash, appropriate to your character, to the entire hand.

Cut under the new fingernail with a scalpel to give it the appearance of a real nail. You will be able to make the nails very realistic with time and practice. Notice the sample hand in the photograph. Once the hands are cured in the oven you may paint on half moons if you want to give the nails a French manicured look.

Be sure when you make the second hand that you have made one left hand and one right hand. The thumb of each hand, when placed by the doll, should point to the front of the doll. If one points forward and one points backward you have made two left hands.

The finishing touch on the hands is done with acrylic paint and china paint powder. If you are making a young person, brush on rose-colored china paint with a mop brush to add realistic color. If you are making an older person, you may wish to paint on age spots and color in the veins. If your doll represents a person who has worked a lot outdoors, you might want to paint the entire hand with a light wash to tint it and give it more of a weathered look.

A nice way to show off a doll's hands is to place them on a musical instrument, as I did on this doll holding a saxophone.

CHAPTER 5
Sculpting the Feet and Shoes

Shoes and feet are among the most exciting parts of the sculpture. They not only form the base for the doll to stand on; they also help set the style of the character. It is very difficult to find ready-made shoes for adult dolls, so making your own is by far the best option. You can make the perfect size and style to fit your sculpture. It is possible to sculpt a wide variety of shoes, ranging from sandals to cowboy boots to old-fashioned high-heeled lace-up boots. When making your own shoes, you are limited only by your ability to sculpt.

In addition to sculpting your own size and style of footwear, you may also sculpt the shoe to indicate that the character is walking, sitting, standing or even kneeling. Some dollmakers like to make a shoe-shaped armature and glue very thin leather (the best is from old kid-leather gloves) over the top of the armature. Another alternative is to glue leather over the top of the shoe armature only, and paint the clay sole and heel to match the leather.

The foot armature, which is formed out of aluminum foil, also becomes the armature for the shoe, which is then sculpted on top of the cured foot. To

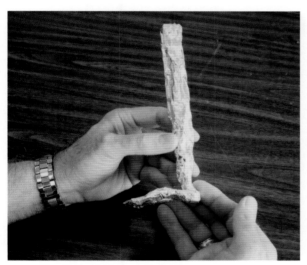

The foot armature is formed out of aluminum foil.

begin making the foot armature, fold a 12-by-18-inch piece of aluminum foil into the shape of a bread stick. Roll the foil from the long end so the finished bread stick shape is 12 inches long. Measure two inches from one end and bend into an L shape, which forms the basic foot. Bend the leg forward just above the heel to form a round ball on the back of the foot. Form the arch, instep and toes from the foil. The toes are formed as though they were inside a stocking; you needn't put in each toe. Using a four- by four-inch piece of foil, make a very soft ball. Place the ball in the space between the instep and the leg on the upper part of the

foot. Form the foil to make the shape of the instep, thus helping to make the shape of the foot. Bend the leg backward at the half-way point just below the knee. Fold the leg backward until the end of the fold touches the heel. This forms the calf muscle and the Achilles tendon. Then form the entire foot by pressing the foil tight until it looks like a finished foot. Keep in mind that this is a foot armature, not a finished foot, and will be thinner than the finished foot. Still, the more the armature looks like a finished foot, the more accurate your foot and shoe will be.

Wrap the heel with floral tape in a figure-eight, as

To form the calf muscle and Achilles heel, bend the leg backward at the halfway point just below the knee. Wrap the heel with floral tape in a figure eight, as if you were wrapping a sprained ankle.

if you were wrapping a sprained ankle. Then wrap the entire leg from the top to the bottom. Pull the tape, stretching it as you apply it to the foot. The process of pulling the tape releases wax from the tape and helps it stick to itself. The tighter you wrap the foot, the better the clay will stick to the finished armature.

Using a dowel made of wood, shape the aluminum foot until you are completely satisfied with the shape. Be sure to make the second foot opposite from the first, so that you have a left and a right foot. It helps to look at an illustration of the profile of a foot in your anatomy book, or even to take off your shoe and examine your own foot as a model. Remember, the finished foot is only as good as your armature.

If one foot is slightly longer than the other, cut the excess foil with a pair of scissors. If it is too wide, crush the foil until the shape is as you like it. If it is too narrow, add another piece of foil to the foot and re-wrap it with paper tape.

Form the arch, instep, Achilles tendon, toes and the calf muscle until you are satisfied with the shape. The left and right foot should be the same length, height and width. To determine the proper length foot for your figure, place the heel of the foot on the chin of the head and pointing towards the hairline. When you measure, remember that your armature is slightly smaller, and narrower, than your finished foot will be. The finished foot with the clay on it should reach from the bottom of the chin to the top of the head, and the width should be the same as the palm of the hand or half of the face.

You are ready to apply the clay. Make a ball of clay about the size of a plum. Roll the ball into a long coil; flatten it into a thin piece of clay about 15 inches long and 1/8th-inch thick. Lay the flattened coil around the foot starting at the top, and moving down the foot until you have covered the entire foot. Make sure not to over-lap the clay as you lay it side by side down the foot. (Overlapping the clay will make the skin of the foot too thick.) Smooth the clay with your thumb until it is all one piece from the top of the foot to the bottom. Make a flange (stitch button) at the top of the leg to help attach the body stocking to the leg. Stand the foot upright on a cookie sheet and place it in the oven at 275

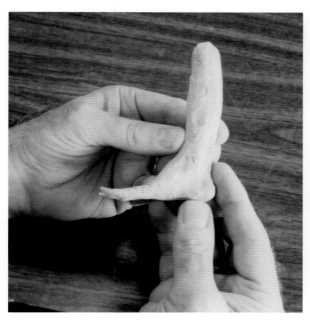

The wrapped foot armature is smoothed and ready for the clay to be applied.

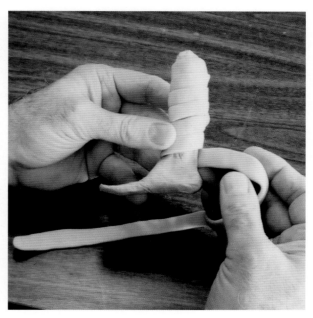

Apply the flattened worm of clay to the armature.

degrees for ten minutes. After the foot has cured, let it cool before removing it from the cookie sheet. The body parts are very susceptible to cracking while they are hot, so it is best to let them cool to room temperature before taking them off the cookie sheet.

To make a more advanced foot that holds a hidden doll stand, add a 3/16th-inch brass tube inside the middle of the foot and leg. Pushing a hole through the foot and leg with an ice pick before you put the clay on the foot creates a tunnel for fitting the brass tube into the foot. Once you have made a hole all the way through the foot and leg, insert the brass tube through the foot and leg, starting at the heel and going all the way to the top of the leg. Then follow the steps above for applying the clay. Glue the brass tube inside the leg for stability. Later the brass tube will fit over a rod placed in the wooden base and the body armature. The illustration on page 62 will help you better understand how the hidden stand works.

While the foot is curing and cooling, make the pattern pieces for the shoes. Make two balls of clay, each about the size of a plum; flatten each one into a pan-

The clay has been put on and smoothed.

cake about 1/8th-inch thick. Cut out two headstone-shaped vamps for the top of the foot (refer to the illustration on page 58). Each one should be two-and-half inches long and one-and-three-quarter inches wide. Then cut out two rectangular pieces of clay, called the counters; each one should be two-and-a-half inches

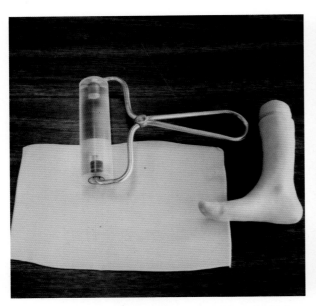

*Roll the clap out into a flat sheet, 16th-inch thick
and measuring four by six inches.*

*The pattern pieces for the shoe are cut out with an
Exacto knife.*

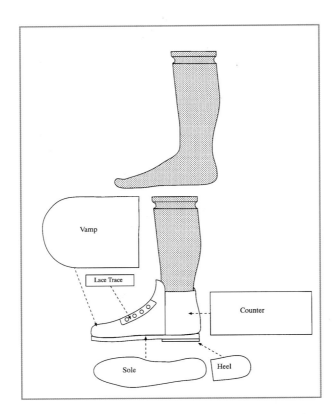

long and one inch wide. Make the sole by placing the foot on top of the thin clay and cutting around the foot to make a foot-shaped pattern. Cut it about 1/8th inch wider than the foot in order to have enough clay to make the sole for the bottom of the shoe.

If you are making a boot, you will also need to make the upper part of the boot in the shape of a two-by-two-inch square. You can see both the regular shoe and the extension of the upper part for a boot in the illustration at left.

Lay the vamp on top of the instep and smooth the sides down over the foot. Cut the excess clay from the bottom of the foot to keep the foot from getting too thick. Lay the counter around the heel and cut away the excess clay where it joins to the vamp. Seam all of the clay together into one smooth piece of clay. The reason for putting the clay on in sections is to make sure that the clay is the same thickness for the entire shoe.

If you are making a boot, put the upper portion of the clay around the leg and seam it to itself and to the top of the vamp and counter. If you are making a Mary Jane, or a loafer-style shoe, cut the excess vamp and counter away until the remaining clay looks like the shoe you are making. Cut away all of the clay that doesn't look like the shoe you are making.

Lay the sole on the foot and seam it to the bottom

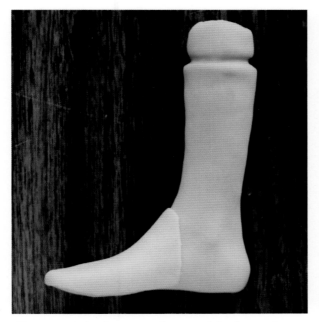

The vamp is in place over the top of the foot and toes.

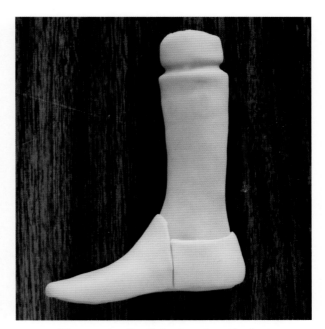

The counter (heel) is placed on the foot.

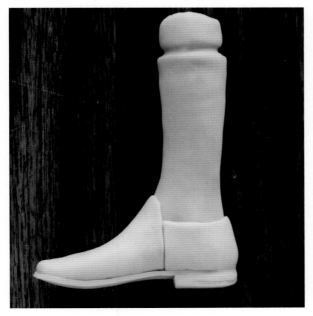

The sole and heel are put on.

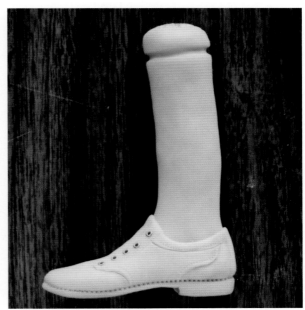

The shoe has been styled with seams and stitches.

of the vamp and counter. If you keep the sharp edge of the sole where you cut it, it will save time and work later. Put on the heel, taking care to give it a finished look by using the primary sculpting tool and a knife.

Styling the shoe with seams may be done by pulling the detail tool over the surface of the wet clay, gently scoring in the seam lines. Smooth the shoe with your thumb and primary sculpting tool until you are satisfied with the shape.

Put in any holes for laces after you have smoothed the surface and lined in the seams. The laces will be put in the shoe after it is cured and cooled.

Detail may be added alongside the seams with the pounce wheel. Use the small-size wheel to create the

The lace holes and laces are in place.

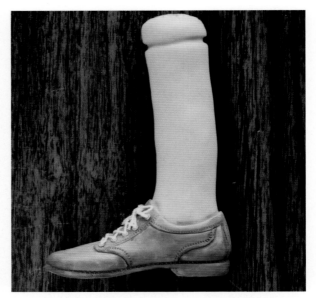

The shoe has been painted with an acrylic wash.

appearance of sewing stitches and the large tool to create the appearance of a sewn-on sole and heel. Looking at the photographs will help you understand which of the pounce wheel tools to use, and where to use them. Since you are the designer, you may use the seams and stitch marks anywhere you wish on the shoe, but keep in mind that the seams and stitches are there to assure the shoe fits on the foot, as well as to make a more pleasing design. The stitches and design should be realistic in their placement. I recommend using a real shoe or a photo of a real shoe as your model.

Now that the shoe is smoothed, it is ready to be painted. Use a thin wash of color to cover the shoe. Let it dry completely before putting on the second, and any subsequent, coats of paint. The first thin wash puts a primer coat on the clay, which allows the second, and any subsequent, coats to dry properly. Putting the paint on in thin coats assures that the paint dries and also helps create an antique look for the surface of the shoe. Once the shoe is painted, paint the sole with a contrasting color. Once the shoe is completely painted and dried, you may wish to antique or stress the shoe by brushing a lightened color over the toe and heel. This process is done with a very dry brush. The antique

brush marks add a very realistic highlight.

The finishing touch is to add an off-white or light-brown color to the stitches around the sole of the shoe. Paint a very thin line of color over the pounce wheel stitches to make them appear to have been sewn with thread. If you do this right, you will fool even the most critical consumer eye. I have had people marvel at the realistic shoes on my dolls. Once a judge marked me down at a professional show, remarking that I used a shoe that I had purchased from a commercial vender. When I explained the shoes were clay and not leather, she re-judged my doll and I won "Best of Show."

Continue painting the shoe with other colors until you like the finished color and style. Notice in the photo on the opposite page that I have put a two-tone color on the shoe and then a light stain over the finished shoe with a very light brown wash. This creates a nice antique look.

Using a purchased doll-size sock, place it on the finished foot and cut it off just above the foot and heel. Once you have cut away the foot portion, pull the top of the sock over the leg down to the shoe. Using white glue, glue the top of the sock to the leg so that it looks as though it is tucked into the shoe. If the foot and shoe

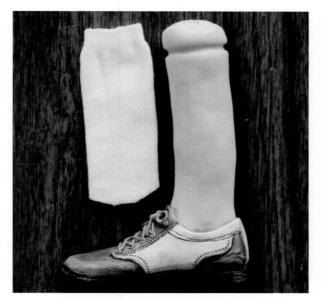

The two-tone painting is complete; it is time to make the sock.

The sock is glued to the leg just above the shoe.

The shoes and socks are finished.

To insert a hidden doll stand, drill a hole through the heel and up through the leg.

are already attached to the body, pull the sock over the shoe and then up the leg until the sock appears to be in the proper place, then glue it as described above.

If you wish to create a more advanced shoe with the hidden doll stand, you will have already drilled a hole through the heel, the foot and up the leg. If the

brass rods you use are long and go all the way up to the neck of the doll it will stand on one foot without any problem.

If you want to put your finished shoes and doll on a base of wood, drill a hole in the base with a 3/16th-inch drill bit and then insert a 3/16th-inch brass rod. Place the

A brass tube fits inside the shoe.

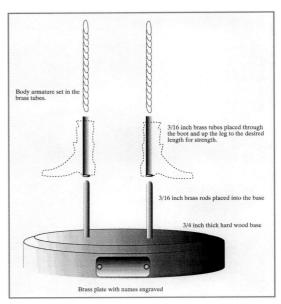

This illustration shows the hidden stand process.

Body armature set in the brass tubes.

3/16 inch brass tubes placed through the boot and up the leg to the desired length for strength.

3/16 inch brass rods placed into the base

3/4 inch thick hard wood base

Brass plate with names engraved

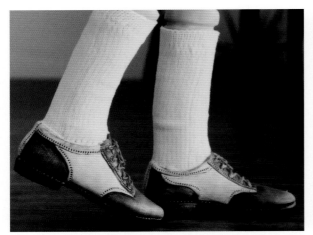

The shoes are posed in a walking fashion.

Drill into the stand to accommodate the brass rods.

shoe containing the 3/16th-inch tube down over the rod, and the shoe will be firmly attached to the base.

To make the doll appear to be walking, bend one of the legs at the knee. You should make this decision before inserting the brass tubes and rods, because you must only put the brass tubes and rods in the straight foot. Once the tubes and rods are inserted, the leg cannot bend.

If your shoe requires texture for realism, choose an object with the texture you would like on your shoe. Press the textured item into the wet clay. For example,

I made the cross-hatched edge on the tennis shoe shown on the opposite page with the edge of an Exacto knife; you may also use a pounce wheel to achieve this effect. Make the upper part of a tennis shoe look like canvas by imprinting a broad cloth fabric or a piece of soft canvas into the wet clay.

Put every detail you want into the finished shoe and smooth it completely before putting it in the oven. Cut away any excess clay on the sole and heel with a sharp knife before putting it in the oven. Anything you smooth out or cut away now will save you time and

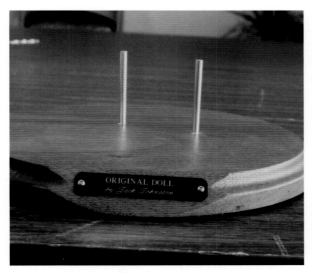

The brass rods fit in to the drilled holes.

The shoes fit easily over the brass rods.

The tennis shoe has a realistic texture.

The finished boot features spurs made of clay.

work after the shoes are cured. Put the shoe in the oven at 275 degrees for ten to fifteen minutes. When curing a shoe, I sometimes leave it in the oven longer and at a higher temperature (up to 300 degrees). The extra time and temperature may make the clay a little darker, but it also makes the shoe and leg much stronger and helps prevent breakage of delicate parts like spurs. As you are going to paint the shoe, it won't matter if the foot is a little darker. (I do not recommend over-curing the other extremities, as the resulting color is not attractive.)

Once the shoe is cured and cooled, you may sand

it with fine sandpaper to help shape the shoe, sole and heel. After sanding or cutting the excess clay away, you will need to smooth the area with fine sandpaper and then paint the sanded area with a Q-tip dipped in lacquer thinner or acetone. Be sure to use the lacquer thinner or acetone in a well-ventilated area.

An advanced shoe-making option is to add an accessory to the shoe or boot. For example the cowboy boot shown above has a set of spurs added for realism. The spurs and the leather strap holding them on were all sculpted out of clay, just as the boot was.

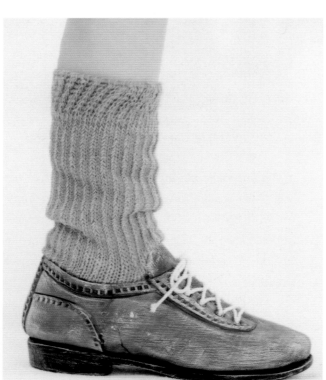

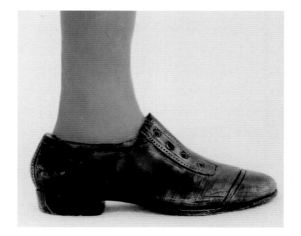

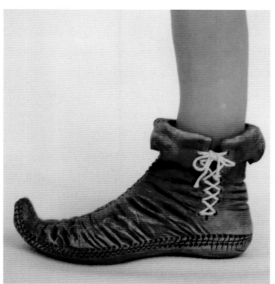

CHAPTER 6
Creating the Soft-Sculpted Body

The artdoll really starts to take shape once you make the body and put on the head, hands and shoes. Making the body is rewarding; it serves as the combining element that ties the parts of the sculpture together. When the parts are all put together, you put gesture into the body, add the costume and bring the doll to life.

Start with the body stocking and armature. I advise starting with a pre-made body armature and body stocking (both of which are available in retail shops); this will save you hours of time sourcing the materials and then making your own. With a body stocking in hand, simply put the pre-made armature inside the body. Once the armature is inside, bend the arms straight out, as though you were making a scarecrow. The legs will be spread apart wide enough for you to be able to stuff the body with polyfill. Stuff the body from the top of the neck, putting in enough polyfill to fill out the body. Do not overstuff it; put in just enough to fill all the voids inside the body. I like the filled body to cover the entire wire armature and to feel much like a loaf of fresh bread.

Once the body is stuffed, you must sew it up. The first stitch is made using a three-inch needle and a three-foot piece of upholstery thread. Anchor the thread to the crotch of the body stocking by using what is called a tailor, or a French, knot. With the thread anchored to the crotch run the thread inside the center of the body to the top of the buttocks. Push the needle through the body stocking at the top of the medial fold (the crack between the two cheeks of the buttocks) and down over the body, back to the original anchoring point. Re-anchor the thread and pull it hard to form the medial fold. In this way you will form two very well-pronounced cheeks. With the thread still attached, run the thread under one of the cheeks over to the side of the body, then up to the hipbone, where you should anchor it. After it is anchored, bring the thread back over the top of the thread you just attached and anchor it in the center of the crotch. Make the other cheek just as you made the first. When both cheeks are finished, anchor and cut the thread.

The next anchoring point is under the armpit. With the thread securely anchored, take it around the arm to the top of the shoulder (high on the side of the neck) and make a basting stitch through the side of the neck. Continue with the thread until you have gone all the way around the arm. Anchor at the base of the armpit again. Using the same thread, go through the torso and anchor at the other armpit. Make the other shoulder just as you made the first one. Anchor at the base of the armpit and cut the thread.

Next, form the breasts by anchoring in the center

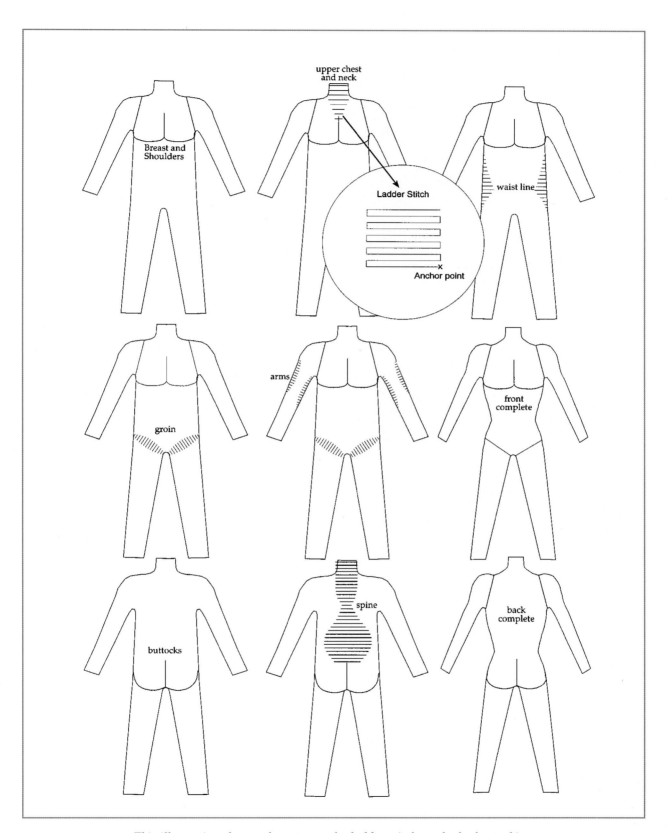

This illustration shows where to use the ladder stitch on the body stocking.

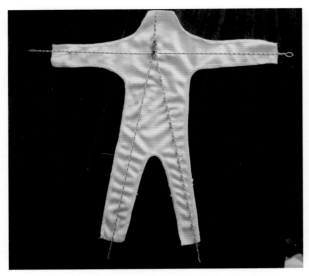

The body stocking is ready for stuffing.

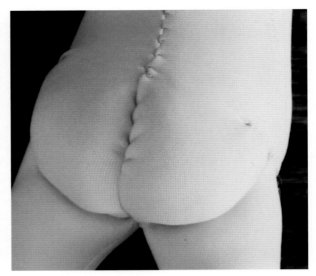

The stitching shapes the buttocks.

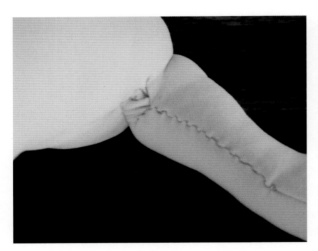

The second anchoring point is under the armpit.

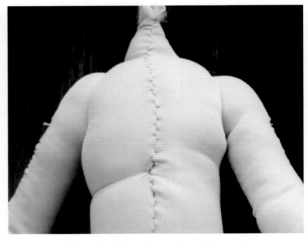

The shoulders have been formed.

of the back at the same height level as the base of the armpits, or at the eighth lower thoracic vertebra. After you have anchored on the back, run the needle through the body of the doll and come out in the center of the chest, at the same height level as the base of the armpits—the sternum—and anchor again. Now, run the thread on the outside of the body from the center of the doll under the breast to a spot one-inch below the armpit and anchor again. This forms the pectoralis major under the breast. This is the same for a male or a female. After anchoring one inch under the armpit, go through the body, come out at the other side and

anchor once more. Now, take the thread on the outside of the body under the second breast, forming the second pectoralis and then anchor in the center of the chest. With both breasts now showing cleavage, cut your thread.

If you wish to have more perfect breasts showing, insert prosthesis breasts. Form a round ball of clay the shape of a breast. Flatten the back of the breast to help it fit into the chest of the doll. Using the brown clay, put a nipple on the front of the breast. Cure the breasts in the oven. After they cool, place them under the skin of the body stocking, positioning them to your liking. For a

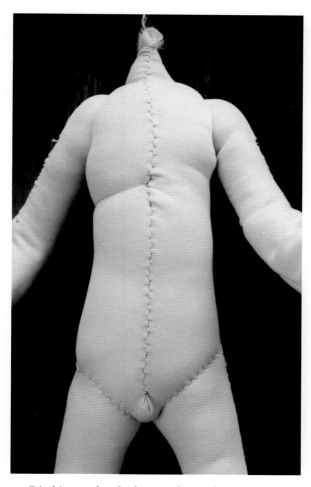

Stitching under the breasts forms the pectoralis.

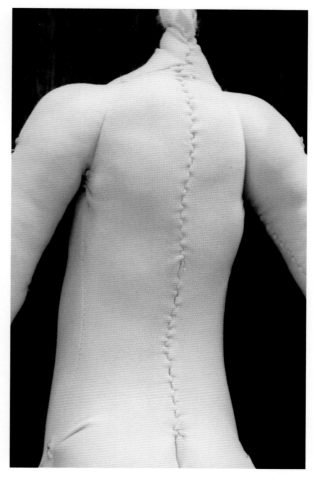

The ladder stitch forms the back bone.

young person, the nipples should point up; for an older woman, they are more likely to point down. To create pendulous, sagging breasts, push them down lower in the breast pocket. The breasts will be held in place as you tighten the body with the ladder stitch up the back.

Before stitching up the back of the doll with what is called the ladder, or hidden, stitch, you must make a series of dots outlining where the stitches go. Using a disappearing-ink pen, make a series of dots leading from the top of the buttocks up the back to the top of the neck, in the form of an hourglass shape. The dots at the top of the neck should go out to the side seams of the body stocking. Once the back and neck are sewn all the way up to the top of the body stocking, the two seams will be drawn together, making a pointed neck. This will enable you to put the finished head over the

neck armature and body stocking. The dots will disappear within a few hours (depending on the humidity). You may wish to follow the photo on this page when making the dots on the back of your doll body, to assure the right shape.

Once the dots are in place, anchor at the top of one of the cheeks. After anchoring, draw the thread across the body to the other cheek and make a basting stitch (go through the material, but do not anchor). From this basting stitch, go back across the body to the next dot on the other side of the back just above your first anchoring point and make another basting stitch. Repeat this, going up the back until you have run out of thread or come to the waist, whichever occurs first. Pull the thread tightly; notice that the back comes together as though you were tightening a corset.

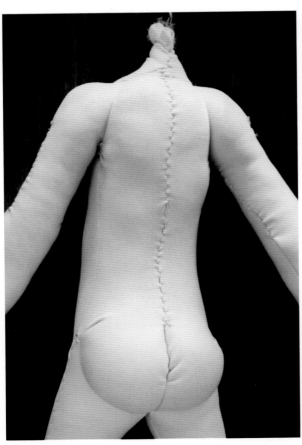

When the thread is tightened, the back takes shape.

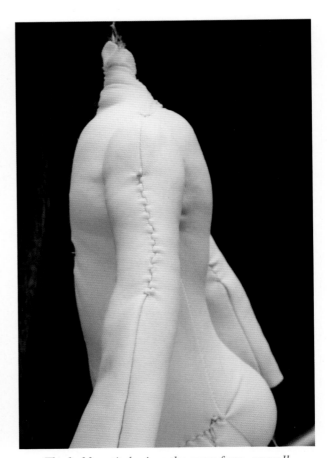

The ladder stitch gives the arms form, as well.

Without anchoring again, keep stitching up the back, going from dot to dot until you have reached the top of the neck. Once you reach the top of the neck, again pull the thread to tighten the stitch all the way up to the neck. The fabric at the neck should come to a point; anchor it tightly. If you have done this stitch correctly, it will form the backbone and add shape to the back of your doll body. This stitch is almost magical in that it not only pulls the pieces of fabric together, it also shapes the spine of the doll in one pull of the thread. Many artists describe it as one of the most exciting parts of making the doll's body.

With the backbone complete, draw dots on the chest from the bottom of the breast to the top of the neck. Now, sew up the chest with the ladder stitch all the way to the top of the neck. This makes a point out of the neck and gives you a place to put the head (which you will do later).

Next you must ladder stitch the top of the arm, using the same ladder stitch as on the back and the chest. Run the stitch from a point one inch below the shoulder on top of the arm to the elbow. Once you have the first arm finished, repeat the same stitch on the other arm. Then, go under the arm and make a dart leading from the armpit out to the bottom of the arm at the elbow. The ladder stitch on top of the arm and the one under the arm, as seen in the photos above, will make the arm thin and much more realistic.

The groin is next. Mark dots leading from the hipbone across the front of the doll to the groin in the shape of a French-cut bikini. The ladder stitch will start at the top of the hipbone, go down across the front of the doll to the crotch, and then up the other side until it reaches the hipbone, as shown in the illustration on page 67.

If you wish to make your doll thinner, add more ladder stitches to the body in the areas you wish to

The lower limbs are attached to the body.

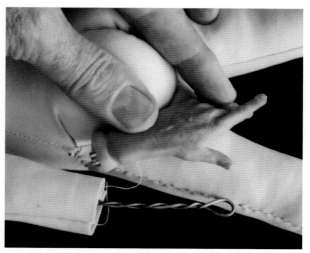

The hands are attached to the body armature.

make thinner. This hidden stitch (taught to me by Mimi Winer) is a wonderful way to make gussets and darts to shape any body you desire on your doll.

The final stitch is putting in the belly button. Place an anchoring point at the top of the medial fold of the gluteus maximus, the position of the coccyx (the fold between the cheeks of the buttocks). Once your stitch is anchored, go through the torso and come out at the navel or belly button, just opposite the fourth lumbar vertebra. Anchor at this point and pull the thread tight to make a nice deep navel. The tighter you pull the thread the deeper the navel and the flatter the stomach becomes. It is often said that the male navel is lower than a female's navel, but my research does not indicate any difference.

Now you are ready to attach the head, arms, legs and shoes to the body. Start by measuring the length of your doll by using the head as the measuring tool. A doll representing an adult in the prime of his or her life should range in height from seven-and-one-half to eight heads tall. Place the head on the neck and then count the body height from the top of the head to the bottom of the feet. The perfect body should be eight heads tall, however, it is not unusual for an older person to be as short as six-and-one-half heads tall. So, for example, if your head is two-and-one-quarter inches high, multiply that by eight. Your doll should be 18 inches tall. Most dolls made from the pre-made head armatures I recommend will range from 18 to 20 inches in height.

The width of the body at the shoulders is two heads wide, if the heads are lying down. If the heads are standing upright, the width of the body at the shoulders is three heads wide. There is one head length between the bottom of the chin and the top of the nipples. From the nipples to the navel is one head length. From the navel to the crotch is one head length, and from the crotch to the bottom of the extended fingers is one head length. From the fingertips to the bottom of the knee is one head length, and from the bottom of the knee to the top of a man's stocking is one head length. From the top of the stocking to the bottom of the foot is one head length. Use the illustration on page 24 to help you measure from the top of the head to the bottom of the feet.

Measure down four heads from the top of the skull

to the top of the hand. Cut the rounded end off of the pre-made metal-wire armature and place the forearm and hands on the metal armature by inserting the wire into the brass tube of the pre-made hand armature. Once you are satisfied with the measurement, cut the wire armature to the length you like and use hot glue to fix the hand to the armature. I recommend hot glue because if the hand isn't right or it later breaks you may remove it from the body by blowing hot air against the forearm with the heat from a hair dryer. With the hands and arms glued to the body armature, pull the cloth of the body stocking down over the stitch button flange and tie the sleeve down with a piece of strong upholstery thread wrapped over the body stocking over the top of the flange. You may either turn the body stocking inside the sleeve and put a hidden stitch around the wrist, or turn the sleeve out and tie a piece of thread around the sleeve to hold it in place. If you roll the sleeve up it will look like an undershirt with the sleeves rolled up. Select the method of tying it off depending upon whether or not you plan for the costume the cover the arm all the way down to the wrist. Once you have tied the body stocking sleeve to the arm, you may wish to cover the attached area by wrapping a piece of leather three inches long and one inch wide around the arm. Glue the leather around the arm to finish off the sewn attached area. The photo on page 71 will help you better understand how to attach the arm. With the arm attached, use the ladder stitch to seam up the body stocking to make it fit the arm perfectly. If there is a void of polyfill in the arm, add more by stuffing it into the arm with a pair of hemostats until you like the shape. Sew it to the desired shape using the ladder stitch.

Attach the head and feet. Attach the head by placing the neck down over the body and armature. Press it firmly down on the body to see if it fits. When you are confident it fits properly, put a fair amount of hot glue into the neck cavity and then place the head on the body. Turn the head to one side to give it a little more gesture. Hold it down firmly against the body until the

glue has cooled and the head is completely anchored.

The hot glue will be cured and hardened within five minutes. Once the glue is hardened, you may bend the head on the wire armature. If you ever need to remove the head from the wire armature and the body stocking, you may do it by blowing hot air towards the neck. It should take about five minutes of hot air to

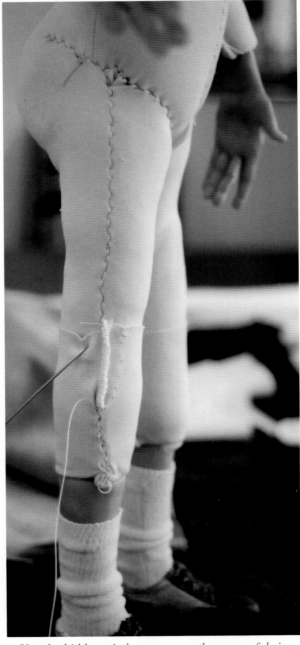

Use the hidden stitch to seam up the excess fabric.

release the hot glue and allow you to remove the head. Put the head back using the same steps as when you first attached the head to the wire armature.

Once the head, hands, and feet are attached to the body, pose the doll. Pose the arms by bending the metal armature at the shoulders and at the elbow; do not bend the polymer clay, as it will break. Bend the backbone

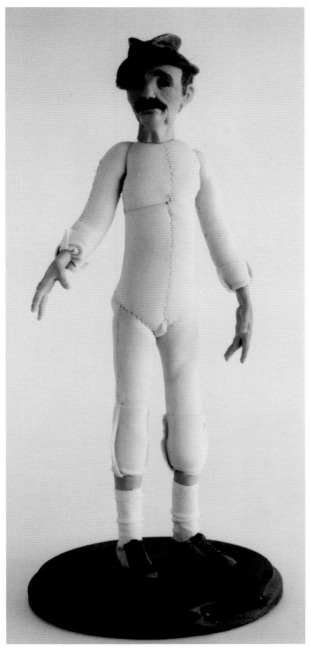

When the head and limbs are attached to the body armature, it is easy to pose the doll.

to help your doll sit, stand, lie down, walk or run. To show aging in the doll, round the backbone. For the doll to sit, bend the legs at the bottom of the buttock and again at the knee. Bending the arms close to the body enhances the realism of the overall gesture. You may wish to bend the head up or down, depending on the gesture you want the doll to make. As the head is glued firmly to the armature and body stocking, it should be able to be posed very easily—up or down or from side to side. Once the doll is posed, though, I try to leave it that way for the rest of its life. If you change the shape too often, you may fatigue the metal and break off an arm or leg.

The body you have just completed is called the 1,000-stitch body. There is an even more advanced body called the 2,000-stitch body. The 2,000-stitch body is made in a fashion very similar to the one you've just completed; the only difference is that once the body stocking is sewn to completion, you add a nylon stocking over the top of it. To do this, cut three very small holes in the toe of the stocking. With the arms of the body extended upward, pull the stocking down over the body, putting the arms and the neck wire through the small holes you made. The stocking will fit tightly over the torso. Cut the bottom of the stocking from the bottom of the feet up between the legs to the crotch. Sew the legs up the inside as you see in the photo on page 74. Repeat the steps you used to make the breasts and the medial fold, but this time use a brown carpet thread that matches the nylon stocking. Notice that the thread does not show, yet the contours are clearly shown. Make the arms by cutting a square of nylon fabric from the stocking and sewing it to the under garment at the shoulders and on the inside of the arm.

The 2,000-stitch body should be used primarily by professional doll makers. The only advantage of putting the nylon stocking over the finished body and adding the additional stitches is that it makes a perfect body. If you want to show off a bare stomach, bare buttocks or bare breasts—for example, if you are making a belly

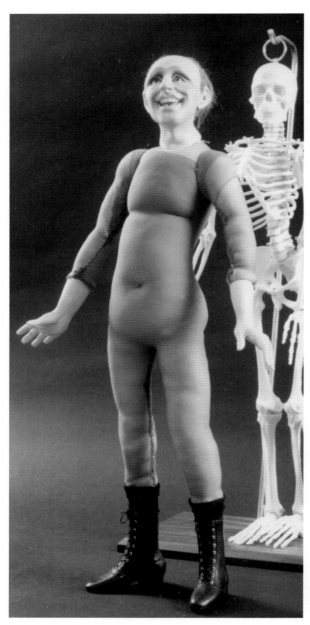

The 2,000-stitch body is intended to be made by advanced dollmakers.

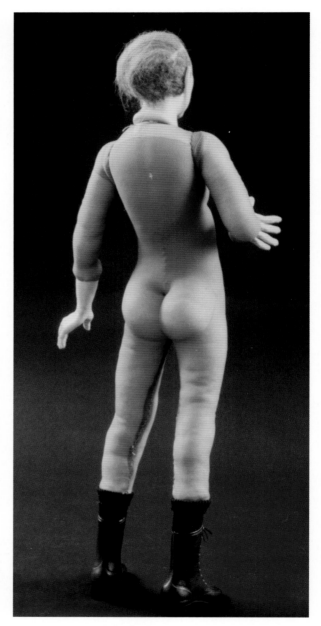

A rear view of the 2,000-stitch body illustrates the realastic level of detail that can be acchieved.

dancer—the 2,000-stitch body is the best method to use.

An even more advanced body is the full sculpt armature. When executed properly, it allows you to sculpt a full figure. To make the body, use the same armature you used for the soft body. Make a wooden base out of a piece of pine ¾-inch thick and cut it into a nine-by-nine-inch square. Into the wooden base, drill two holes of the

same diameter as the legs on the armature. Put a leg armature in each hole; this allows the armature to stand upright while you wrap the body and sculpt the figure. Wrap the wire with aluminum foil to form the legs, arms and torso. Attach the hand armatures to the body armature as described in the chapter on hands. Fashion a head and neck out of aluminum foil, and attach them to the

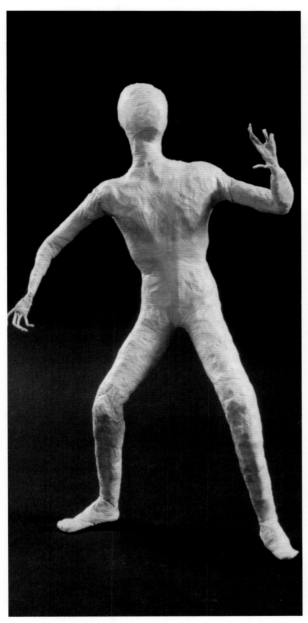

The full sculptured armature involves applying aluminum foil and then clay over the entire body.

The rear view shows the fully sculptured body armature before the clay is applied.

neck wire and the shoulders of the body. Once the aluminum foil is in place, wrap the entire body, arms, legs and head with floral tape. Since this body has a wire armature inside and is standing erect on the wooden base, it may be posed anyway you like.

Apply clay over the entire body; adjust the final pose. Once it is sculpted and cured it will always stay in that pose. If the doll is small enough so to stand upright in your household oven for curing, leave it on the work base and put it in the oven. If it is too tall, take it off the wooden base and lay it in the oven for curing. Lay it on polyfill and cure it face up for 15 minutes at 275 degrees. Let it cool completely, roll it over and cure the other side for 15 minutes at the same temperature.

CHAPTER 7
Costuming

Costuming the doll may be as simple or as complicated as you like. The degree of complication depends on whether you sew or glue the seams of the costume together. I use a combination of three methods: machine sewing, hand stitching and gluing. The rules of most professional doll shows state that the "Artdoll should appear to be undressable." The word "appear" is the key word. Judges of antique and porcelain dolls like to examine the dolls' costuming all the way down to the underwear. Judges of artdolls are pleased just to look at the dolls and assume they have underwear, functioning buttons and (what appear to be) real zippers. If your artdoll appears to have real buttons and zippers, that will be fine at most contemporary doll shows. You should check the rules of the show before you enter your sculpture to be sure you have complied with their rules.

To help you understand how to make a simple costume I asked Diana Stover, a master dollmaker from the Professional Doll Makers Art Guild, to demonstrate a few techniques on her sewing machine. She used a finished artdoll as the mannequin. With the brass tubes in the shoes and legs of the doll, it stands up quite firmly on a wooden base.

When choosing fabric, you should select the thinnest material you can find. I like to use a fabric from a worn piece of clothing, because it is already soft and should hang correctly. The older and thinner the fabric is, the better it will hang on the doll. New fabric is full of starch and does not hang properly.

Before cutting your actual fabric, you should always cut a pattern out of muslin or another inexpensive fabric. Muslin also makes a great pattern for later use, as you can write all over this material.

If pants are part of your costume, start by making them. A pair of pants may take one-quarter of a yard to make, so be sure you have more fabric than you need. Drape the fabric from the waist down the leg to the length you desire. Mark the top and the bottom of the fabric to the length you have selected. Now cut the shape illustrated in the simple patterns on the opposite page to make the crotch, waist and legs.

Mark the length of the pants on your pattern fabric, and cut out the shape of the leg. Once you are sure the pattern fits the doll, you may cut the fabric you plan to use for the costume itself. For these pants, we chose an old chambray shirt for the jeans. Pin the chambray legs to the mannequin by putting a pin through the cloth and sticking it right to the body of the doll.

Next, sew or glue the two pants legs together at the crotch and down the inseam of the legs. With the pants sewn or glued together, take the doll off the stand and

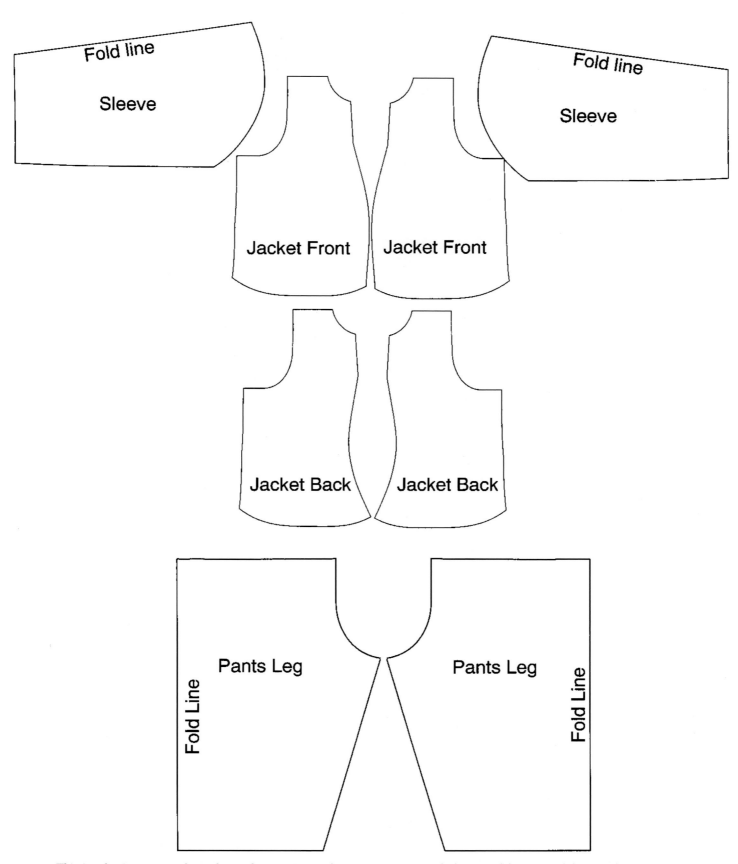

This is a basic pattern of a jacket and pants. Most of my patterns are made from modifications of this simple pattern.

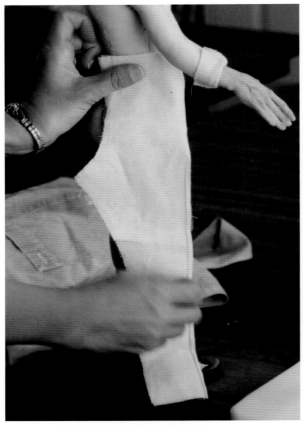

Hold the pattern up to the doll.

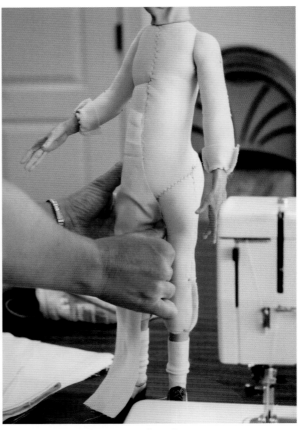

Adjust the pattern length as necessary.

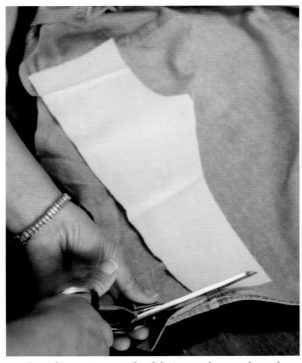

Lay the pattern on the fabric you have selected

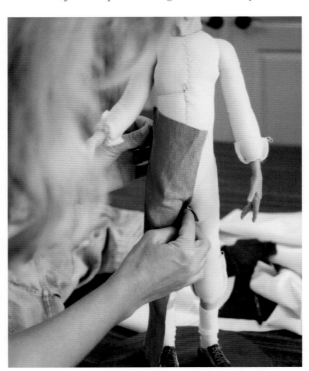

Drape the actual fabric piece over the doll.

Pin the legs to the doll.

The doll models his pants.

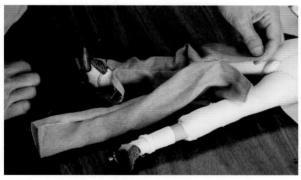

Put the pants on the first leg.

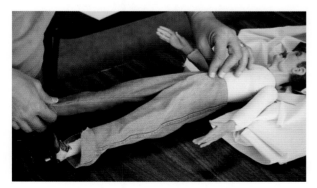

Put the pants on the second leg.

put the leg and foot through the pants leg to see that it fits properly. If you need to make simple alterations, this is a good time to do so.

Put the doll back on its stand and pull the pants up to their finished position. You may pin them in to place for now (later you will tailor them to fit perfectly).

The shirt is made from an old plaid shirt. I've also chosen the smallest print I could find. (When I purchase a new shirt for myself I always think of using it when it wears out as fabric for making costumes for my dolls. Therefore, I always try to buy thin materials with a small print.)

Follow these simple patterns to make your own. First create a cloth pattern from muslin or another inexpensive fabric to fit your doll. Drape it over the doll to make sure it fits. You may pin the fabric together to hold it while you drape it over the shoulders.

Once you are satisfied with the way the cloth pat-

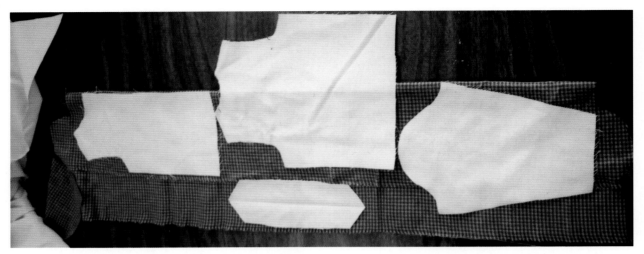

Once the cloth pattern pieces are pinned together (below left), lay them over the fabric for the shirt.

Before laying the cloth pattern pieces on the fabric (above), pin them together.

Sew the sleeve to the body of the shirt.

Hang the shirt on the doll to size it properly.

Sew the cuffs of the sleeves.

Sew the collar together at the base.

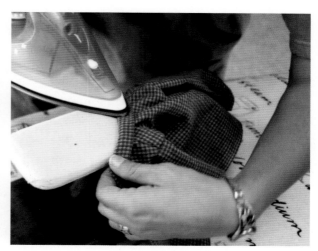

Iron down the collar.

It is best to sew on the buttons by hand.

Use the ladder stitch to tailor the pants.

tern hangs on the doll, cut your actual fabric. For the back of the shirt, place the pattern over folded fabric to assure that the pattern for the sleeve cut outs are the same on both sides. Do the same for the front of the shirt.

Sew or glue the tops of the shoulders together, and then do the same with the sleeve. The cuff for the sleeve is a simple piece of fabric folded to look like a cuff, and then sewn or glued onto the sleeve.

Hand sew the cuffs on the shirt to assure they fit properly and are very strong. You may do the same with glue, however I recommend sewing the edges at least, so they stay while the glue dries.

The collar is made of one piece of cloth folded over, and sewn or glued together, then turned outside in. Tack the collar to the shirt with a sewing machine or by hand.

Iron the costume as you make it to assure that the collar, sleeves and cuffs all fit as nicely as possible. You should also iron the entire shirt once it is finished. Once it is on the doll you will not be able to iron it again (although you can steam it straight if necessary).

I have found that the only proper way to put on a button is with a needle and thread. The glue does not hold the button well, and it is nice to see the thread holding it into place.

You are now ready to tailor the pants and shirt to fit the doll perfectly. Use the ladder stitch shown in

Chapter 6. This stitch will allow you to tailor the pants to fit the waist.

Hold the neck together by sewing on one of the buttons. This also allows you to tailor the shirt to fit perfectly. Hold the tips of the collar down with glue. I use fabric glue because it is washable, pliable and will hold forever.

Next, make the sweater from an old sock. This is the perfect time to use that one sock that was found in the dryer. (Never throw out an odd sock again; you can always use one to make a sweater for your doll. The smaller the print, the better it will fit the scale of the doll.) If you want a special print or knit, you may have to purchase a new pair of socks, but that is still a relatively inexpensive way to get a sweater for your doll.

Cut the end of the sock off at the top of the foot as shown in the photo above. Cut the shape of the neck line and two holes for the arms to go through. Pull the sock over the doll from the feet up, and sew or glue the top of the shoulders together. To make a better edge, roll the edges of the fabric under and sew or glue them down. The bottom edge of the sweater is formed from the top of the sock as it was before you did any cutting. Making the sweater is so easy that it doesn't really take

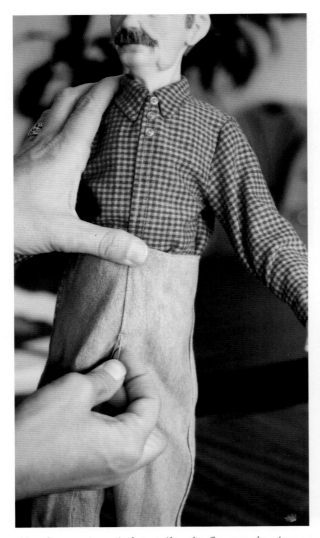

Use the running stitch to tailor the fly over the zipper.

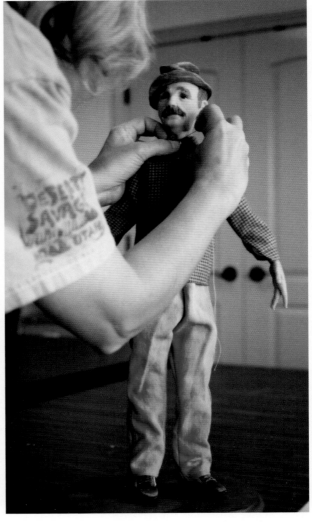

Sew on the buttons to hold the neck together.

Cut the foot off of a sock.

Sew or glue the shoulders together.

The costume, made by Diana Stover, is complete.

Jumpin' Jack Flash has a collar and shirt that is merely a dickey.

The Old Pioneer Lady's dress is made from the long sleeves of a full-scale lady's blouse.

a great deal of explanation.

Notice in the photos of the completed costumes that the neck, cuffs, sleeves and waist are all tailored to fit the doll exactly. Store-made clothing for a doll will never fit like tailor-made clothing will.

If you don't like hand sewing the costume, you may use Fabri-Tac glue. I recommend Fabri-tac because it glues very quickly, stays pliable and is washable. Once the basic trousers and shirt have been placed on the doll, you may add such things as cuffs, belts, outside pockets, etc. If the doll has an undershirt, I put it on as dickey—meaning the undershirt is really only around the neck and the end of the arms, not under the entire over-shirt. For example, the collar and shirt shown on the cover doll, Jumpin' Jack Flash,

detail above left, are fake—they are only for show, yet they look real. Nor do I line the jackets or the trousers. Lining only bulks them up and causes them to appear too thick and out of scale.

To form a miniature dress, I like to use pieces of a woman's blouse. The tucks that are already in the sleeves of a long-sleeved shirt, for example, are perfect for the waist of the Old Pioneer Lady's Dress, above right. The completed waist with the tightly tucked fabric was the sleeve of the full-size blouse. The bottom of the dress is the extended sleeve of the blouse. The top of the dress is another sleeve from the blouse. The only part of this dress I had to sew were the sleeves. Everything else was already made in the original blouse.

Aaron wears a sweater made from an old sock.

To look realistic, a belt should actually work.
This one is made from a watchband.

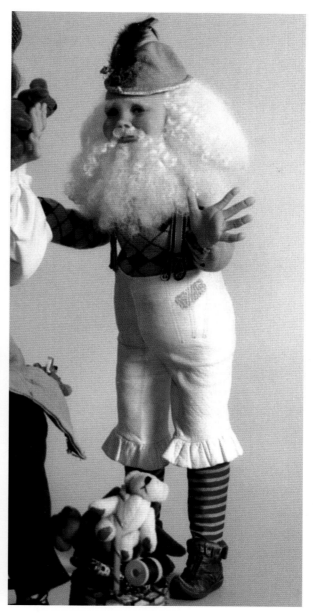

An old kid-leather glove was used for the Elf's bloomers.
The ruffled top of the glove serves as the bottoms.

The sweater on Aaron, above, was made from a child's winter sock. Cut the foot off of the sock, put two holes in the side of the sock near the top to slip the arms through and pull the sock over the head of the doll. As you pull it over the head, put the arms through the two small holes you cut in the sides. The top of the sock becomes the neck of the sweater, and the rest of the sock becomes the body of the sweater. Cut small rectangular squares of some additional sock material, and sew or glue them to the body to form the beginning of a sleeve. Sew up the backside of the arm with a ladder stitch to tailor the sleeve to fit the doll. This is the fastest and best way I have found to make a winter sweater for your doll. A child's sock usually has a print of suitable scale for a doll's sweater.

The Elf's costume shown above is made from a kid

leather glove. The ruffled top of the glove serves as the ruffles at the bottom of his bloomers. His sweater is made just as I described above. This costume cost 25 cents for the old sock and two dollars for the kid-leather gloves. The rest of the costume was made from clay and mohair.

The beauty of sewing or gluing costumes together is that they will be tailored perfectly for the doll. Costumes made on a sewing machine often look too big for the doll. If you sew the costume by machine, you must leave the sleeves large enough to go over the hands, the pants large enough to go over the shoes and the neck large enough to fit over the head.

If you prefer to make the complete costume on your sewing machine you may wish to put the costume on the doll first and then glue on the head, hands, and feet. This eliminates the problem of getting the costume over the body parts.

I recommend sewing on the buttons, but not actually making them function. The belts I make work, which helps the overall realism of the costume. (See the photo at right and the detail of Santa's belt on the previous page.) I do not recommend making a zipper that works because it is usually too large for the scale of the doll; instead I make the flap for a zipper and sew or glue it shut.

Clothing such as aprons and vests should be made and attached just as full-scale aprons or vests would be. Remember that the doll you are crafting is one-quarter human scale so the thickness of the clothing should also be one-quarter the thickness of full-size clothing. Using antique fabrics, kid-leather gloves and silks or other thin fabrics is a good way to maintain this scale.

The difference between a great doll and a world-class doll often lies in the accessories. Imagine a cowboy standing in a field, now put a rifle in one hand and a saddle slung over his shoulder. Put a little boy carrying a wooden rifle walking next to the cowboy's side and suddenly the dolls tell a complete story; nothing more has to be said.

Most artists spend at least one day each month looking for accessories. I'm no different in the respect that I'm always looking for that cherished treasure for an accessory. However, there is one difference, I don't look for an accessory to fit a doll, I make the doll to fit the accessory. Of course I also look for accessories that will fit my dolls, but if I find a great treasure, I buy it no matter the scale. If need be, I design a doll to fit the accessory. I once found a wonderful set of salesman's sample snowshoes made in the early 20th century. They were a little larger than I usually use, but they were so detailed, I didn't let their size stop me. I put the snowshoes with Jeremiah Johnson, a character out of our Western heritage. As the snowshoes were so realistic, I felt I had to photograph the doll outside in the wilderness. The scale of the grass and trees worked well in the photograph and the doll looks very realistic.

This Cowboy has a working belt and leather chaps.

Jeremiah Johnson was inspired by a set of salesman's sample snowshoes, circa 1910.

CHAPTER 8
Displaying and Lighting

In my gallery, the sculptures are displayed on four-foot-high pedestals with Plexiglass covers.

Whenever possible, a doll's display should be designed as a permanent site. My sculptures each have a four-foot-high pedestal on which they stand. The pedestal may be made of fine hardwood with mitered edges, or it may simply be plywood covered with Formica. The top covering may be made of glass, Plexiglas or acrylic. There are three good reasons to keep the dolls inside sealed coverings. First, it assures no one will touch the dolls; second, they will not collect dust, and third—they simply look better! If a collector can afford to own one of your one-of-a-kind artdolls, he or she should be able to afford to properly display it.

Proper lights are as important to the display as is a

The display case may be glass, Plexiglass or acrylic.

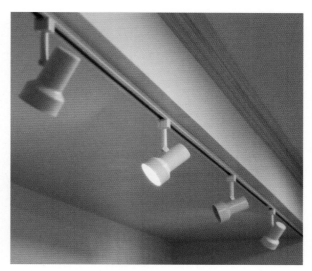

Track lighting includes several lights that can be aimed at the dolls.

proper display case. If budget is not a factor, there should be three spotlights on each doll: two lights at quartering angles above the doll and one at the base of the doll's feet. The best lights to use are mini all-spectrum spots. The all-spectrum spotlights will bring out the true color of the doll and its costume. The worst kind of light to use is florescent, as it brings out the greens in the doll and diminishes the reds. If you are building a new home or a special room for your sculptures, you should have canister lighting put in the ceiling above each doll.

In most cases you will likely be displaying your sculptures in a home or office space that is already built. In this situation, I recommend track lighting. Each track holds several lights that can be aimed at the dolls. Do not scrimp on lighting; when you put up the track make sure they are the right size for maximum effect. If you put up a small track, you will see shadows on your dolls and will most likely want to enlarge the track before too long.

There are situations that require theatrical lighting to create a special effect. Theatrical lighting means a rear lit spot behind the doll, or a single spot directly above or below the doll. Some of the most effective lighting is created by placing hidden spots behind the

doll or in front of the doll, hidden inside one of its props or accessories.

Exciting lighting is the doll's best friend. Lighting can also be the doll's worst enemy. If a doll is exposed to too much light, it will, in time destroy the brilliant colors in the costume. To help avoid harmful ultra violet rays from light, be sure to use UV-protected glass or acrylic cases for your doll. You must also be sure that direct sunlight never gets to your doll. In a perfect world, light should be on a doll only when it is being viewed. I recommend keeping the blinds and the drapes closed in the room where you keep your sculptures.

Temperature and humidity also affect your permanently displayed dolls. Ideally, the doll should never be exposed to extreme heat or cold. The biggest problem with heat and cold is the rapid deterioration of the glues used in the construction of the doll; i.e. hot glue melts at high temperatures and releases at cold temperatures.

The effect of a humid or moist environment may totally destroy the doll within a very few years. Just as any fine piece of furniture or fine fabric must be kept dry, so must your artdoll. I do not mean that the dolls are going to be ruined in your lifetime, but if they are true artdolls they will be passed down from generation to generation, so let's take care of them.

CHAPTER 9
Cleaning, Repairing and Shipping

As long as a doll is kept inside a glass or acrylic case, it will stay clean for years. If it does get a light coat of dust on it, it may be cleaned with an air dispenser. The air-dispensing cans used to clean computer keyboards are the best. The dispenser has a very small straw nozzle that can be aimed at parts of the costume to blow off any particles of dust. A large soft-bristled brush may also be used to brush the face and other hard surfaces on the doll.

To keep the hair in order, it can be combed with a single needle just as when you first styled it. If the hair was originally put on with hot glue and needs to be replaced, remove it with a hair dryer. Aim the air from the hair dryer at the clay at the base of the hair and remove it gently as the glue heats up.

If the hair was put on with fabric glue, remove it with acetone. Take care not to get the acetone on the face, as it will also remove the paint. With a cotton swab, put the acetone on the roots of the hair and let it slowly dissolve the glue. After you have completely removed the hair, wash the top of the head with acetone to remove all of the glue. Once the hair is gone, either put on a fresh wig or put on all new hair and style it to your liking, as you did in chapter one.

One of the most common things to happen to a doll is a broken finger. If you put the hand and arm on with hot glue, you're in luck. Just aim a hair dryer at the broken limb and wait a moment until the dryer heats up the glue and then remove the hand. When the hand is off the doll, repair it with fresh clay and re-cure it in the oven.

If you put the hand on with permanent glue, or if you are at a show and a finger breaks, you can fix it without removing the hand. First mend the cracked finger with "super glue." Then sculpt fresh clay over the mended area to completely hide the crack. Use a hair dryer pointed at the new clay to cure it. The air coming out the end of the hair dryer should be at least 250 degrees. The closer you get to the subject you are curing the hotter the air from the dryer will be. For a proper curing, keep the new clay hot for at least five minutes. This process will get you through the show, but when you get back to your studio, remove the hand and make a new one.

I am often asked about the best way to transport dolls. If you are transporting dolls without accompanying them, the best method is to wrap them in bubble wrap, and then double box them. Wrap the head, hands and feet in bubble wrap. Wrap the limbs tightly so they fit tightly to the body and can't bounce around. Once each limb is wrapped, wrap bubble plastic completely around the doll, forcing the arms down tightly to the side of the torso. Wrap the legs tightly together with a small roll of bubble wrap between the shoes so they can't hit

Mark Twain is in the Enchanted Mansion Museum in Baton Rouge, Louisiana.

The Norma Rockwell Triple Self Portrait is in the Franklin Mint Gallery in Philadelphia.

against one another.

With the complete body wrapped like a mummy, lay the doll in a bed of soft shipping peanuts. The box should be approximately three inches longer and wider than the length of the doll. Fill the box tightly with shipping peanuts and seal it with packing tape. Place the box inside a slightly larger box, to give it strength. If you purchase new boxes for your shipment, you will be able to buy boxes that fit inside one another. If the second box is too large to fit snugly over the first, wrap the outside of the first box with bubble wrap and then put it inside the larger box. There must never be room for anything to move inside the box.

The best shipping method is two-day air. This assures that the box is hand processed, and is not at the bottom of a pile of other boxes. Insuring the shipment is a good idea. If it is insured, it will get the same treatment as regular two-day mail, but you will sleep better.

To avoid high shipping costs, you should always pack the doll yourself and take it to the departure site. If you use a packaging service, you are likely to pay three to four times the regular shipping costs. What's more, most packaging services do not understand how to pre-

pare a doll for shipping.

Because you have folded the arms to the side of the doll and the legs to each another for shipping, it is essential to send a photo of the properly posed doll to your buyer. You might also want to include an illustration of how to pose the doll, and an explanation of how to care for it.

If the doll is very expensive and it is important that it is posed with the proper gestures, you might want to deliver it yourself. To assure that my Norman Rockwell Triple Self Portrait, above right, was set up properly, I personally delivered it and set it up. I did the same with Mark Twain, above left. As these dolls sold for $20,000 and $30,000 respectively, the airfare was a small price to pay to assure their proper set up. If you personally set the dolls up at their final display spot, you can also arrange the lighting and placement in the room. If the pieces are kept in a museum or other permanent display, it is appropriate to show the curator or owner how to clean and care for the sculpture. If the location is not terribly inconvenient, you may even want to clean and realign the piece once a year yourself.

CHAPTER 10
Marketing

Once you are making dolls regularly, you will probably begin to think about selling them. To sell your dolls successfully, it is essential to have a well-thought-out advertising and promotion plan. But the first question that comes to most people's minds is usually: "How much should I sell my dolls for?"

Pricing your dolls is based on a simple formula; add the cost of materials plus overhead plus advertising to the value of your time to arrive at a wholesale selling price. The wholesale price is the price paid by retailers or other middlemen, and is usually approximately half of the final retail price paid by collectors.

You should begin by keeping a day-to-day record of your expenses and income. Even a small company needs to know the costs of doing business in relationship to the income derived from sales and other sources of income. There are simple software programs available to assist you in understanding your income vs. expense comparison. The one I use and recommend is Quicken©.

If you analyze your monthly income and expenses you will note that some months of the year are much better that others. The longer you are in business the more accurate your analysis will become. You may find that every June (vacation time) your business slides to the lowest month of the year, yet in November your sales peak, thanks to Christmas. Armed with this kind of information, you can plan your year accordingly.

If you sell your dolls one-on-one to a collector, you should always sell them for retail price, or double your wholesale price. If you sell your work to retail stores, as well, you must always sell your sculptures to collectors at the retail price, or you will upset the stores that carry your work. Retail shops need to sell the dolls at a keystone price (100 percent markup). I know it is hard to understand why the shop wants to make as much money on the doll as the creator does. Remember, though, that the costs of running a business—rent, building maintenance, salaries, advertising and promotion—demand that a merchant mark up the products a minimum of 100 percent. If a merchant were to sell a product at the wholesale price, he or she would essentially be giving that product away. Depending on the costs of running a particular business, the mark-up on a product might go as high as 200 percent of the wholesale price.

Instead of selling directly to retailers, you may choose to sell your dolls to a distributor who will sell to the retailers for you. If you do this, you still sell to the distributor at your wholesale price. The distributor will most likely add 25 percent to the retailer, who then adds a 100 percent mark-up to the price they paid. By the time your doll is on sale at the shop, it is marked up

125 percent from your wholesale price. This is the average mark-up.

If you are concerned that your doll may not sell at the higher marked-up prices, you need to improve your skills or reduce the costs of making the dolls, or both. The only way you can reduce the cost is to work faster, smarter and in volume. Purchase your materials in quantity so as to reduce the cost of supplies. Hire someone who will work cheaper and faster than you to do the tasks that don't require your talent.. You will not only save money, you may also save time in sculpting dolls, because the more dolls you make, the faster you will become.

Besides retail and distributor sales, you should be ready to think about selling doll designs to manufacturers. The price for the right to reproduce your work is considerably higher than the price of selling one doll to a collector, retailer or distributor. A one-of-a-kind doll that sells for $1,000 may sell to a manufacturer for three to five times that amount in advanced royalties plus an ongoing royalty (three to five percent) for as

long as that doll is reproduced.

Generally the original fee for the prototype doll is paid in an advance against future royalties. The royalty amount varies depending on how many dolls the manufacturer reproduces, the materials the doll is made of, and the retail price for which it sells.

If your doll is being manufactured in large numbers for sale to a television outlet such as QVC or Home Shopping Network, the royalty you earn may be as low as ten percent. On the other hand if your doll is being reproduced in a small quantity, such as 25, you may earn a royalty as high as 25 percent. Manufacturers typically base the royalties on net sales, which means the profit after manufacturing costs and returned dolls are subtracted from the gross sales. Gross sales is the number of dolls sold multiplied by the selling price per doll.

For example: A manufacturer pays $20,000 to produce 1,000 dolls of your design. He agrees to pay you a royalty of ten percent of net sales for each doll sold on QVC. QVC agrees to purchase 1,000 dolls from the manufacturer for $50 each, or $50,000.

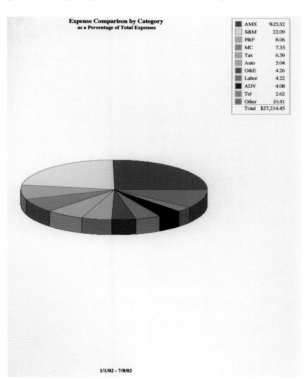

The pie chart shows the costs of doing business.

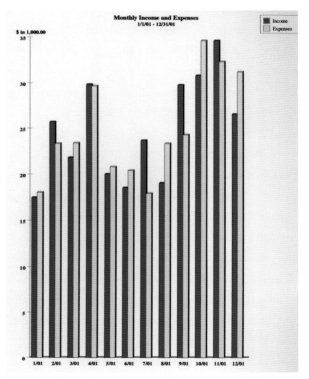

The bar chart shows one year's expenses and income.

During the show, QVC sells 950 of the dolls and returns the other 50.

In this example, the gross revenue is $50,000. The manufacturing costs were $20,000 and the unearned revenue from the 50 returned dolls is $2,500. The net sales on the doll are $27,500 ($50,000 minus $20,000 and $2,500). Your royalty earnings are ten percent of the net sales, or $2,750.

Sometimes the manufacturer also subtracts their marketing costs and research and development costs from the gross sales, further reducing the net sales. This is called triple net, and in such a case your royalty may effectively be only one to two percent of net sales. I recommend you consult an attorney or an experienced business person in the doll industry to read over any contracts you may be negotiating. Most doll manufacturers are honest, but I like President Reagan's philosophy: "Trust but verify."

As a sideline to selling your work on television, you may be asked to make personal appearances on television shows or at trade shows. If you are asked to make personal appearances, make sure your travel and lodging expenses are paid by the manufacturer. We are all flattered to be asked to be on television, but if you have to pay for your own travel costs, they will soon eat up the profit on your doll sales. Be sure that things like appearances and travel are spelled out in your original contract.

Most manufacturers contract to have you make one prototype doll. Once you send them the doll they study it, make changes and send it back to you for modifications. Once they like the finished prototype, they photograph the doll and send pictures around to their staff, companies that buy from them and other knowledgeable doll enthusiasts. If everyone loves the doll, it is sent to the marketing staff for pricing. If marketing says they can sell the doll and the accountants say they can make a reasonable profit on the project, then it goes to production. It generally takes one year from the day a manufacturer signs an agreement with you until the doll hits the shelves. The manufacturer may invest thousands of dollars photographing and testing your doll. They are likely to assign one person to your doll to see that it is properly tested. That person may work on your doll for several months. The manufacturer invests this amount of company work and time when buying your doll design. The only risk to you is that your doll is off the market for at least one year while they do their test marketing. The best thing that can happen is that your doll is a hit. The worst thing is that they return it and say: "it is not marketable at this time." Selling to a manufacturer, television marketing company or a direct mail company may be very lucrative for you. If your dolls don't sell well, you will likely only receive the original advance against future royalties, but it's still worth taking the chance.

Intrinsic value pricing comes at the point in your career when everyone wants one of your sculptures, but there are only a few one-of-a-kinds available. After you have developed celebrity status, a doll that sold originally for $1,000 may sell on the secondary market for two or three times that amount. After you retire, or pass on to the "big doll show in the sky," your sculptures may command 10-20 times their original selling price. I used to laugh at the intrinsic value pricing theory until I tried to buy my original sculptures from my early customers at quadruple the selling price, only to be told they're not for sale. Where were all these high-paying customers when I was selling my first dolls for $129?

Let's recap the preceding information on pricing. The following pricing formulas are standardized throughout the dollmaking industry.

Labor + Materials + Overhead = Wholesale Cost

Wholesale Cost + 25 % Markup = Distributor Cost

Distributor Cost + 100 % Markup = Retail

Retail Price + Advance Against Future Royalty + Ongoing Royalty = Manufacturer's Price

Retail + 200-500 % Markup for "Fame" = Intrinsic value price

Before you can use any of these formulas, you

must first set your hourly wage at a price that you can live with. If you are earning your living making dolls and nothing else, you need to set your annual salary by using the following formula.

Monthly wage divided by the number of hours you devote to your dollmaking equals your hourly wage. Divide your monthly wage by the number of dolls you can make in one month to set the price of each doll.

For example, if you need a $3,000 monthly income and will work 160 hours a month, your hourly wage is $18.75. If you can make four dolls a month, your time for making each doll is set at $750. If you add $250 per doll for general and administrative costs (overhead), then you will set a price of $1,000 for each of your one-of-a-kind artdolls.

I remember a discussion I had with the late Bob McKinley, one of the most famous one-of-a-kind contemporary dollmakers. I asked him the same questions I hear from others today, "how do I price my dolls?" His answer was: "charge enough money for your work to pay your expenses and then raise your prices after you have paid your dues." I never knew exactly what he meant by paying dues until I had been in the business about ten years. I was in an elevator full of people in the Toy Center in New York City and overheard two doll collectors speaking to one another (they didn't know I was in the same elevator). One said to the other, "I must purchase one of Jack Johnston's dolls this year before he kicks the bucket." I realized then that by paying your dues Bob meant putting in the time and work necessary to master your craft. Only then will your work be worthy of higher prices—and only then will collectors be eager to pay whatever they must to own your work.

There are many ways to sell a doll. I have discussed selling wholesale, retail, to distributors and to manufacturers; now let's explore selling your own creations at shows. There are scores of small doll shows around the nation; you can read about their locations and dates in the doll trade magazines. The most important shows are those I refer to as the "Big Four:" The

American International Toy Fair in New York City, The International Doll Exchange (IDEX) in San Francisco, The Doll and Teddy Bear Show in Pomona, California and the Doll and Teddy Bear EXPO in Washington, D.C. Over the years, these shows have proven over the years to be the most professionally run, with the largest attendance and therefore the ones at which you will likely have the greatest success.

The American International Toy Fair is held at the Jacob Javits Center in New York City for nearly a week in mid-February each year. The show is open to the trade only, and not to the public, and is the venue for toy manufacturers to introduce new toys for the coming year. A section of the show is reserved for Collectible Dolls, Miniatures and Plush. This whole-sale-only show is the largest toy show in the United States. It is approximately twelve football fields in size and houses more than 5,000 exhibitors. The gate (number of buyers) ranges from 45,000 to 60,000 retail shop owners. Those attending the show are made up of retailers, distributors and manufacturers, including the major doll manufacturers. Publishers, promoters and doll service vendors also attend. The booths range in size from ten-by-ten feet to 100-by-100 feet. The major doll companies have booth ranging in size from 600 to 2,400 square feet. The cost of the booths in 2003 is 20 dollars per square foot. There are additional charges for carpeting, electricity and cleaning. If you choose to participate in the management's advertising and promotion opportunities, additional payments are required. Because a ten-by-ten-foot booth can cost as much as $3,000, a more practical way to display your creations at Toy Fair is by sharing the booth with other artists. To learn more about Toy Fair, check their website: www.toy-tia.org or call the Toy Industry Association at 212-675-1141.

The International Doll Exchange (IDEX) is held in San Francisco, California, at the Billy Graham Convention Center every January. One day is devoted strictly to the wholesale market; the following two

The Professional Doll Makers Art Guild exhibits in a large booth at Toy Fair.

days collectors are allowed to come in and view the exhibits—though they may not buy directly from the exhibitors. Booths range in size from a single table to ten-by-ten booths to a combination of booths from 20 to 60 feet long by ten feet deep. The cost of the space in 2003 ranged from 200 dollars to approximately 2,000 dollars. The additional costs for electricity and other services are very reasonable. The gate is generally from 4000 to 8,000 consumers. It is a well-run professional show and a good one to cut your teeth on. The show is managed by Sue McCart with co-sponsorship with *Teddy Bear and Friends* and *Doll Reader* magazines. More information may be found by calling 404-378-2217 or going to www.bearexpo.com.

The Doll and Teddy Bear EXPO, sponsored by *Dolls* and *Teddy Bear Review* magazines, is held annually in Washington D.C. in the second half of August, in a major hotel, in the center of the city. EXPO hosts 100 to 200 booths, ranging in size from single tables to ten-by-ten booths to a combination of booths from 20

to 60 feet long by ten feet deep. It is a well-attended show, with a gate ranging from 6,000 to 10,000. EXPO also includes programs, luncheons and club events. One of the most exciting events held at this show is the annual banquet at which the *Dolls* Awards of Excellence and the Lifetime Achievement award are announced and presented. The three-day show is held on Friday, Saturday and Sunday, with Friday dedicated to wholesale customers, and Saturday and Sunday open to collectors. The price of the booths ranges from 550 dollars for a table to 1,450 dollars for a ten-by-ten booth. A premium spot is an additional ten percent. Carpeting and cleaning are included in the rent for the booth space; electricity and other services are available at a reasonable price. You may learn more by going to the website www.jonespublishing.com, or by calling 800-331-0038.

The KM Showorks Doll, Ceramics, and Crafts Show is held in Pomona, California at the Los Angeles County Fair Grounds. The show is held twice a year, in March and again in October. The show is dedicated to ceramics, dolls, teddy bears and crafts. Like the other major shows mentioned in this chapter, it has vendors supplying dollmaking materials and related crafts, and hosts teachers, guest speakers, celebrities and dignitaries. There are approximately 350 booths ranging in size from ten-by-ten square feet to 60-by-10 square feet. The gate is generally from 3,000 to 5,000 doll enthusiasts and collectors. Like EXPO and IDEX, this show is well run and wonderful for small to medium companies. For more information, call 626-732-0595.

Smaller shows are held at locations in many cities across the nation. These shows may only have 1,000 to 2,000 guests, but they are great way to learn about doing shows and getting involved in the industry. If you are not well-known, you will always have a better chance of selling your dolls at these smaller shows, where better-known artists may not be present. They are also a great place to get initial exposure, and charge much less for exhibit space—often no more than the price of one doll of high quality. Generally, experienced collectors and doll enthusiast attend these shows to see new dolls, get to know the upcoming artists and get in on the ground floor of buying their work. The cost to do one of these small shows is well worth the experience, and you may be lucky and sell a few dolls.

Once you are successful at the small shows, you can consider making the investment in one of the "Big Four." I recommend any one of the four mentioned large shows, but I also recommend exhibiting at your first one with a more experienced artist or group of artists. You might join one of the guilds and learn from the experiences of its members. As the founder and Chairman of the Board of the Professional Doll Makers Art Guild (PDMAG), I recommend it highly. There are also several other good guilds and artist organizations that allow their members to exhibit together and will give you the same advantage. Most of the guilds allow you to join their artists at the major shows once you have been critiqued and admitted as

one of the member artists. As a member of the guild, you may go to Toy Fair or other shows and share the cost of the booth. As non-profit organizations, the guilds only charge you your share of the cost of the booth, and advertising, etc. There will always be experienced artists at the booth with you to advise you and to help you sell your dolls. If you are lucky enough to attract a manufacturer or one of the television marketing companies, you will have help in negotiating a contract from the other members and officers of the guild.

Advertising and promotion are actually more important in the overall marketing scheme than your skill as a dollmaker. I've met wonderfully skilled dollmakers who have found it nearly impossible to sell their dolls. I've also met dollmakers with marginal skills as artists, who have great skills as marketers and have made a fortune selling their work. The fortunate ones either have an ability to market their own work or have the good luck to stumble on to someone who understands marketing.

Advertising in the doll magazines is essential to success. The problem is most new artists are short on money and cannot afford advertising. Therefore, a new artist must be sure that the editors of the doll magazines see their work and feature it editorially—which is free. Magazines are always looking for new artists with exciting dolls. So let's talk about getting editorial coverage before we talk about buying advertising.

There are three simple rules to getting your dolls into the magazines. First, make dolls of high quality; second, take photos of high quality; and third, send the photographs to the editor of the magazine. Sounds simple enough, yet many artists never feel their work is good enough for the national magazines. If you don't promote your work, no one is going to do it for you. I'm an artist and, in spite of my long experience, I have the same insecurities you have. Yet over time, my self-promotion has resulted in the publication of my dolls in many magazines, including cover photos of five of them; my name and my own photograph have appeared thousands of times by now. The only way to succeed in this industry is let people know you exist.

The photographs you send to the magazines for publication must be of the highest quality. The best investment you can make in your career is to hire a photographer of high quality, who knows how to take good photos of dolls. Magazine editors love to discover new talent. If the new talent sends them great photographs of great dolls, the editors will do all they can to feature your work,

The best way to show off your work is to have it photographed with a large-format camera, so that the result will be a transparency at least two and one quarter inches square. Even better is a four-by-five transparency. When photographing your dolls, be sure that they are on a plain background; seamless photographer's paper of a neutral color—blue, gray or tan are good—is best. You want to be sure to focus the viewer's attention on the doll, not on any distracting background. Even fabric can be distracting, with its wrinkles and folds.

Lighting should be even and dramatic, but not shadowy or too soft. You want to be sure that every detail of your doll is in clear focus and can be seen. Show the full figure, without any fancy cropping. An additional close-up of the face is also useful.

Getting your work on the cover of a magazine is a little more difficult for a newcomer, but still possible, especially if your photo is of excellent quality. If you leave enough background around the doll for a magazine's logo on top and coverlines around it, the editor's mind just might begin to visualize a cover when he or she looks at your photo.

Another thing to remember when aiming for the cover is to send your photographs to the magazine at least six months in advance of the print date. For example, if you are submitting a photo of your Santa Claus for a cover, you must send it to the editor in July. Most magazines have a lead time of three to six months; in other words the Christmas issues are planned in the

summer and on press by October. Remember, though, that many magazines insist on using cover photographs that are related to a story inside the magazine. So while your doll may be excellent and your photograph of perfect quality, an editor may have to turn it down until he or she is ready to do a feature story on your work. Some magazines do count show reports as articles from which they may pull cover photos, so if you are exhibiting at a major show, you should be sure to send magazine editors good photos of the pieces you are exhibiting, with a note inviting them to visit your booth and see the piece "in person." Editors like to know ahead of time that there are good photo possibilities from which they can choose to illustrate their show report. If you don't get a cover, you might still get nice coverage in their show report.

If you wish to be write for the magazines, it is helpful to have a specialty as far as subject matter, or a special angle on a common subject. If you have developed a new method of making hand armatures you may suggest writing an article showing your method through photographs and illustrations. Most magazines have editorial guidelines that outline how they like to have articles submitted, whether as manuscripts, or discs or via electronic mail. The editorial guidelines also state how many words the articles should have (a word range, usually), whether or not you must submit artwork, and—most importantly of all—what kinds of articles the magazine is interested in receiving. Before approaching a magazine, study several earlier issues carefully to get a sense of what kinds of stories are published, the style in which they are written and overall lengths.

Many editors prefer to receive a query letter first, outlining the article you would like to write, your qualifications for writing it, and inquiring about their interest in buying the story. A query letter also saves you time and work; if an editor tells you they have too many articles on a certain subject already, you can send the query letter on to another magazine right away. If you do send a full manuscript without a query letter, be

Contemporary Doll *magazine featured*
The Jazz Player on its cover in 2000.

Doll Makers *magazine selected the piece called*
Maurice, The Doll Maker for one of its covers.

sure to include a cover letter introducing yourself, giving a brief description of the article you are submitting and your credentials for writing it. Do not forget, if you are submitting by mail, to include a self-addressed stamped envelope with the proper postage for return of your materials. This is proper publishing etiquette, and has been followed by writers for decades.

It's helpful to the editor if you write in the same computer format the magazine uses. For example, if you work on a Mac computer and the magazine editors all work on PC-compatible computers, you should try to save your material in both formats.

You must understand that if your article is bought, the editor will have complete authority to change and edit it to fit the magazine's style, format, length and other needs. An editor may also ask you to revise or add to your article before or after it is accepted for publication.

Also be sure to ask whether the magazine is buying all rights to the article from you, or only first-time North American serial rights. If it is buying all rights,

the publishers will be able to do anything they wish with your article in the future, including reprinting it in books or other issues and selling the right to reprint it to others. If they only buy first-time North American serials rights, they are buying only the right to publish the article for the first time in a publication in this country. Once the article is published, you have the right to do whatever else you choose with it.

Buying advertising space is costly, but very important. Be sure to research the magazine before buying advertising to be sure it is the right place for your doll to be seen. If you make one-of-a-kind contemporary dolls, it is not a good use of your money to advertise in a magazine that focuses on antiques or reproductions of antiques. Look closely at the articles and other advertisements in several issues of a magazine before you decide to advertise. Call the advertising representative and request a media kit, which should include a sample issue and all the information about advertising rates, and about their readers. Know and understand

An advertisement for Santa and Mrs. Claus ran in Better Homes and Gardens.

your audience before you spend money on advertising. This means you must only advertise to those collectors who collect the type of doll you make. Advertising is common sense; it was once said, that the definition of marketing is: "find out what people want and make it easy for them to buy it."

When buying ad space start with a small ad in one of the national publications and test the water. You can place your ad for less than the cost of one of your dolls. If the ad works then you may be ready for a full advertising schedule. The best ads are the ones that tell the consumer to do something. Never show a picture of your doll and say: "send us a self-addressed envelope and we will send you a free picture of this doll." Guess what will happen—they will all send you a self-addressed envelope asking for a free picture, but they won't buy anything. Your ad must say: "order this doll today!"

Knowing when to advertise is just as important as knowing where to advertise. It has long been said in the advertising business, that you "go hunting while the ducks are flying." It is a waste of money to advertise while consumers are on vacation. It is also a waste of money to advertise a Santa Claus doll in December. If you're advertising in December, you're too late for Christmas sales. Your ad for Santa must be in the magazines in September and run through November. If you have a hard time creating and buying advertising, I recommend that you ask someone who loves to do it for advice or help.

Selling their own dolls is very difficult for most creative people. It is so hard for an artist to impose himself or herself on someone else that many would rather put their dolls on the shelf and starve rather than ask someone to buy them. If this is how you feel, don't feel like you are a failure. If you can afford to have someone else market your dolls for you, that is the best solution. If you can't afford it, and must do it yourself then let me offer you a simple way to sell your work without actually asking the consumer to buy it. I call it the "alternate choice close." Show the customer your dolls, tell them what they are made of and how you made them—that should be easy for you, and enjoyable. By telling them how you made it and what it is made of, you establish a value in the mind of the consumer. For example, point out that it has glass eyes instead of acrylic eyes, that the hair is mohair, not acrylic, and that it took you 40 hours to hand craft the sculpture and costume. Then, rather than saying: "would you like to buy my doll?"—which are difficult words for any artist to utter—say: "I have this doll for $595 and this one for $995. Which is best for you?" You didn't have to use the horrible word "buy" or even the four-letter word "sell." Whichever answer you get from the customer, both choices are in your favor. Finally, notice I priced the dolls at $5 less than the next hundred. In most consumers' minds, this price means they are spending $500 and change, not five dollars less that $600. I didn't come up with this idea, of course, it's as old as merchandising itself. But it's still a good one, and it works.

Two Success Stories: Mark Dennis and Reva Schick

Success in the dollmaking industry can be very sweet indeed. If your dolls are well accepted by collectors, you may be on the ride of your life. It doesn't happen often but it does happen occasionally. For example, the piece Pygmalion (two views shown above) is based on a Greek myth of the sculptor who creates his own perfect woman. Just as the woman comes to life in the sculpture, so has its creator Mark Dennis. Mark was the winner of the 2002 Annual ProSculpt Scholarship award. As one of my students, Mark traveled with us to New York City to show his work at the American International Toy Fair. His honor also brought his work to the attention of *Contemporary Doll* magazine, which featured his dolls. During my years as a teacher, I've taught more than 29,000 students how to sculpt artdolls. Out of the many I have taught, scores have made it to the top. With enough practice, you will achieve just as Mark has.

Baby Girl on a Wooden Horse is by Reva Schick.

Reva also made this Boy with Truck on Bench.

I remember receiving a telephone call from the membership chairperson from The Professional Doll Makers Art Guild (PDMAG). She said she had received photos from an amateur dollmaker in Canada by the name of Reva Schick, who had read my book and was making dolls of polymer clay. The artist wasn't having any luck selling her dolls. In fact she even tried to rent them one year to a local department store for Christmas, but nothing came of it. She was desperate to have her work seen and sold. Her last attempt to become recognized was to call our Guild.

When I saw photos of her work, I called her immediately. In our first telephone conversation I told her I was very impressed with her work and that I wanted her to be a member of the Guild. I told her that not only did I want her to become a member of the Guild, but that I wanted to help her sell her dolls at the American

International Toy Fair in New York City. She was so excited that all she could do on the phone was cry. I'm so emotional that I also cried. Once we had gained our composure, I asked if she could go with us to the Toy Fair in three months. She told me that she and her husband were both out of work, and that going to the Toy Fair sounded wonderful, but was out of the question financially. I asked her if she would be able to get to New York if we didn't charge her anything for the booth space and membership to the Guild. She said she would be there.

When time came to meet at the Toy Fair her sisters-in-law showed up on opening day with two of her dolls, explaining that Reva's father had died the day she was to leave. They had brought her dolls for me to see and sell. I telephoned Reva and told her not to worry because I would take care of everything. I asked

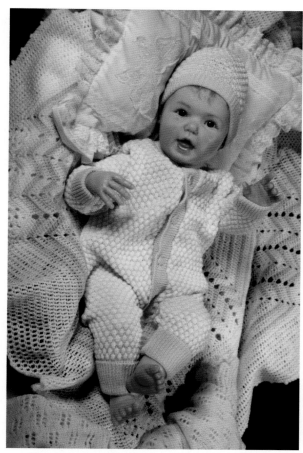

Timmy is the doll that launched Reva's career.

her how much she wanted for her dolls, and she said to sell them for anything I could get. I told her I would set a price and try to find a manufacturer to carry her dolls. I further told her that as president of the Guild, I would sell her dolls and negotiate the contract with no charge to her. She agreed and gave me carte blanche to sell and negotiate a deal with a manufacturer.

The first day the show opened I took orders for 18 dolls at $1,250 wholesale each. I also showed her dolls to three manufacturers: Ashton-Drake Galleries, Marie Osmond through an anonymous company, and The Lee Middleton Company. All three manufacturers loved the dolls and wanted to negotiate a deal. I told each of the companies that I needed a commitment from them then and there. Marie Osmond loved the dolls and agreed to purchase them through the anonymous company that was manufacturing and selling her dolls at

that time. I told the other two companies that we had made a deal with someone else and thanked them for their interest.

I called Reva and told her of the success we had. She and I cried together again for another few minutes before we made our next plans. As I had donated all of my time, it was now time for her to take the lead and take the next step. I told her to call the manufacturer, tell them of my conversation with Marie and arrange to meet with them for contract negotiations. She called me back within the hour and said she had just called the manufacturer and that they told her they weren't taking on any new artists. I found out later that this manufacturer was in financial trouble and was filing for bankruptcy. Marie had no knowledge of their problem and was brokenhearted that they couldn't live up to her agreement. Marie was frustrated, but the matter was out of her control. Reva was shocked and I was madder than hell. I told Reva I would call The Lee Middleton Company and see if they were still interested, which they were. They called her immediately and arranged to fly her and her husband to their plant in Ohio. Just one week later Reva called me from Ohio. She said they wanted her to sign a contract, told me the terms and asked me what to do. I said, "Sign." I also told her that she was in for the ride of her life.

She signed, she did go to the top and the rest is history. Thanks to our good friend Carole Russell, the director of new product development at the Lee Middleton Doll Company, Reva soon became a star. Reva Schick has become one of the most successful and famous baby-doll artists in the history of the industry. I will respect the confidentiality of her agreement and not tell you how much she agreed to make as income, but I will say that Middleton has sold millions of dollars worth of Reva's dolls. Reva and her husband will never have to worry about income again. This is the Cinderella story of the century for a dollmaker. As I said, it doesn't happen often, but it can happen.

Gallery of Dolls

Where do you get the idea for a doll? How do you find the right accessories? How do you tell a story with a doll? How did you do that? These are some of the questions both artists and collectors ask me. The best way to answer them is to show some of my dolls and tell a little bit about how they came to be. So I have put together a gallery in print of some of my favorite pieces, along with some of the behind-the-scenes stories of their creation.

◆ ◆ ◆ ◆ ◆

The Music Man was made for the Disney World Doll and Teddy Bear Convention in 1991. This doll was auctioned off at the Disney Annual Auction that year for $1,200, and got more publicity than anything I made in those early years. I think of it as the doll that really started my career.

I decided to make **Mark Twain** and then have furniture made to fit his vignette. I contacted a good friend of mine, Dennis Dugan, and asked him to make a roll top desk, a book hutch, a swivel chair and a coat rack. Dennis made all of the accessories, including the coal oil lamp on the desk, from scratch. The furniture cost $5,000 to make, but it made this $20,000 doll come to life. Without the accessories and the vignette, Mr. Twain would not have been the same. This doll was so successful that I decided to make the **Norman Rockwell Triple Self Portrait** with a complete vignette, too.

When I decided to make the **Norman Rockwell Triple Self Portrait**, I traveled to Stockbridge, Massachusetts, to visit Mr. Rockwell's museum. After visiting the museum and negotiating for the right to make the **Triple Self Portrait**, I asked for permission to photograph Mr. Rockwell's studio and painting easel. This was against the rules, but they did allow me to draw the furniture. This was actually more than I had hoped for. I was allowed to sit in Mr. Rockwell's chair and draw the very easel on which he painted his own Triple Self-Portrait. I spent several hours drawing the furniture in his studio and felt very close to him and the marvelous work that he did during his life. I had never met him, but somehow I feel that he approved of what I was doing.

The drawing I did of his easel, stool, bucket and

helmet are based on the actual pieces used in his own self-portrait. There are actually 116 pieces in the vignette. I sculpted the helmet on top of the easel and made the glasses; my wife found a cap on her hairspray that worked for the glass for his drink, and I asked Dennis Dugan to make the easel and the mirror. Everything from the matchsticks on the floor to the illustration on the canvas had to be created from scratch. I drew the portrait of Mr. Rockwell with pencil; I bought small tubes of acrylic paint and used the paint for the tray in the easel and the pallet. I then placed the empty tubes in the trash (of the vignette) and on the floor just as he did in the real painting.

While I was researching the famous paintings of Rembrandt, Albrecht Durer, Picasso and Van Gogh that hang on Mr. Rockwell's easel, I discovered that the one of Van Gogh is reversed from the original painting. Mr. Rockwell wanted the viewer's eye to move from the drawing of his rendering on the canvas up the mall stick to the top of the canvas, then move down the famous artists to Van Gogh and back into the center of the painting. For the viewer's eyes to go back into the painting, he must follow Van Gogh's gaze. Mr.

Rockwell was a genius to even think of such a thing, much less completely repaint the portrait of Van Gogh in reverse and still get a perfect likeness. It was much easier for me; I just took the picture out of the book, put it in the computer, reversed it digitally and printed it on an inkjet printer in the size I needed. I think Mr. Rockwell would have been proud of me for catching him with such a clever change in the original painting of Van Gogh.

Completing the **Triple Self Portrait** took me over one year. I traveled to Stockbridge five times before I finally got permission from the Rockwell family and the museum to do the sculpture. I also traveled to Philadelphia to get permission from Time-Life for the rights to reproduce Mr. Rockwell. Once the sculpture was finished I took it to the 100th birthday party at the Rockwell Museum in Stockbridge. I then took the finished sculpture to New York City to show it at Toy Fair, where The Franklin Mint purchased him for reproduction. Once that contract had been signed, I flew it to Los Angeles to be filmed for a video that Franklin Mint was making. Then I flew it back to Salt Lake City and took it apart for making the molds for reproduction. The sculpture was then flown back to California where the molds and body parts were made. The furniture flew to Asia, where the furniture was reproduced to the exact specifications of the Franklin Mint. Once the furniture and mold were made, the doll and all 116 of its pieces were sent back to me in Salt Lake City to be reassembled into a finished vignette. I then flew it back to Philadelphia and the Franklin Mint Museum where it rests today. The doll traveled nearly as far in one year as Mr. Rockwell did in his lifetime.

As proud as I am of the **Norman Rockwell Triple Self Portrait**, I would like to sculpt it over. I could do it so much better today. I would like to recall all 2,500 reproductions of the doll and sculpt them again. On the other hand, in my more lucid times I remember the amount of work that went into making it the first time, and I think it is better off left alone.

Other sculptures have been exciting for me, too; the 15½-inch **Aviator** is one of my favorites. I found a wonderful replica of a 1945 P-51 airplane pedal car, with no one sitting in it, in a store in California. As it was out of scale for any of my dolls, I made a full-grown man sitting on the outside of the plane, pretending he was flying. As a young man, I had always wanted a P-51 fighter plane pedal car exactly like the replica I found. I spent a lifetime flying 5,500 hours as a multi-engine pilot, so airplanes are a very important part of my life. The **Aviator** is really an "alter ego" of myself and my love for airplanes.

Abraham Lincoln in **Freedom for All** was sculpted for Senator Orrin Hatch. Some 28 years ago I was asked by Senator Hatch to be his pilot and the marketer for his race for the United States Senate. We spent one year together flying from town to town in Utah, "stumping" on the wing of the airplane at every stop. Orrin used to talk to me about his fascination with Abe Lincoln, and discuss why he thought Mr. Lincoln's work was so important to our nation. Orrin has devel-

oped an appreciation and love for American sculptures, paintings by Western painters and my historical figures. The sculpture of Lincoln with the freed slave boy holding the American flag now rests in the Senate chambers in Washington, D.C. I posed Mr. Lincoln's hands in a praying position, and then the only prop this vignette needed was the American flag. The rest of the story is told in history.

The characters in this one-of-a-kind musical crew are immediately recognizable, but **Miss Dolly Parton and the Muppets** wouldn't quite be the same without their musical instruments. Kermit's banjo, the violin and the guitars are all perfect replicas. Each of the replica instruments is so well done that if you photographed them out of scale, you would be convinced they were real.

My Great Grandmother as the **Grand Dame** doesn't need much of an accessory. The umbrella was used as a walking cane; it helps to emphasize the strength of her pioneer heritage. Although you can't see them, she has cowboy boots on under her elegant floor-length dress. This is one of my early sculptures, yet it remains one of my favorites. I've kept her in my collection just to remind me of where I came from and where my journey as an artist has taken me.

Jumpin' Jack Flash is one of the few sculptures I've done that relies on its pose as the prop or accessory. The sculpture is standing on one foot in a dance pose; this allows him to tell his story without any help from additional props. His face has become a part of the logo for my ProSculpt clay. He is also the cover doll of this book.

The **Samurai Warrior,** 14 inches seated is a good example of the costume itself being the accessory. This turn-of-the-century costume was purchased in Japan by Jean Nordquist, the owner of Collectible Doll Company.

I was teaching for Jean in Seattle and when she saw me admiring the costume, she offered it to me if I would make a doll for it. I jumped at the chance and created a sculpture from Creall Therm to adorn the costume.

Boyhood Dreams is a 15-inch Cernit sculpture that says a lot with just two simple accessories; a toy airplane in his hand and a sling shot in his back pocket. This is an alter ego of myself when I was about nine years old. I was raised on a farm near Dodge City, Kansas. The closest neighbor to our farm was three miles away. Since there was nobody nearby to play with, I used my imagination to keep myself busy.

The Santa featured in my seventh video is called **The Red Santa Costumed Doll**. It was made in front of the camera in a two-hour feature film that demonstrated exactly how to make a Santa doll. It was also used in the filming of *Making Santa Claus with Jack Johnston*.

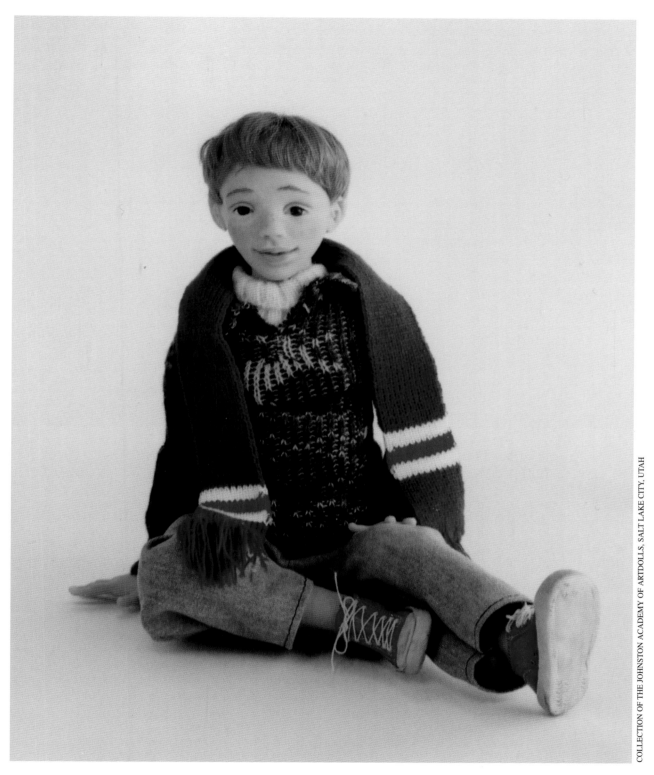

This doll was made as a portrait of my son **Aaron** for my new film, which is entitled *Making Costumes Easy and Cheap*. The costume made for this doll was constructed from old socks and a chambray shirt of mine, which I had worn until it was tattered at the cuffs and collar.

The Navajo Weaver, 12 inches seated made from Cernit has a rather elaborate accessory vignette that demanded the piece be shown in a natural environment.

I filmed the sculpture and the accessories in a dirt field behind a new construction site in Salt Lake City. She seemed quite at home in the desert environment.

Santa and Mrs. Claus may be the most elaborate vignette I have ever put together-or should I say the most elaborate hoax I have ever made? The sculptures are the only elements in the photograph that are in the same scale. This photo was taken to show how to make a vignette using different scales of furniture and background. For example, the fireplace and windows are human scale, the floor is nothing more than contact paper on cardboard and the lighting effect of the fireplace on the costumes is achieved with a spot light right behind Santa. This elaborate photographic set was created using three light sources from different directions. There is a chapter dedicated to this photo in my book *The Advanced Art of Making Artdolls*.

In the close-up of **Santa**, I've put the candles in his hand. Notice how the reflection of the candles on his face gives the doll a realistic look. This set has been published in scores of national magazines and was featured in two television shows.

The Violinist has become famous because of his red hair. Playing musical instruments was a passion of mine through secondary school years and on into college, where I played in the symphony. When I found these wonderful violins I had to make a doll. The color of the violin called out loudly for a red-haired musician. This doll is one of my favorites. He is kept in the Gallery at the Johnston Academy in Salt Lake City, and has his own story. As a young man, Aundrey Ibenkostli, (a fictitious character) learned to play the violin. He loved his music and even developed the skill of making violins. As he improved as a concert violinist, it was certain that he would become world famous. But this was not to happen. Because of his red hair, the aristocrats who attended the concerts did not accept him. As a result, he was held back from becoming a concert performer for the rest of his life.

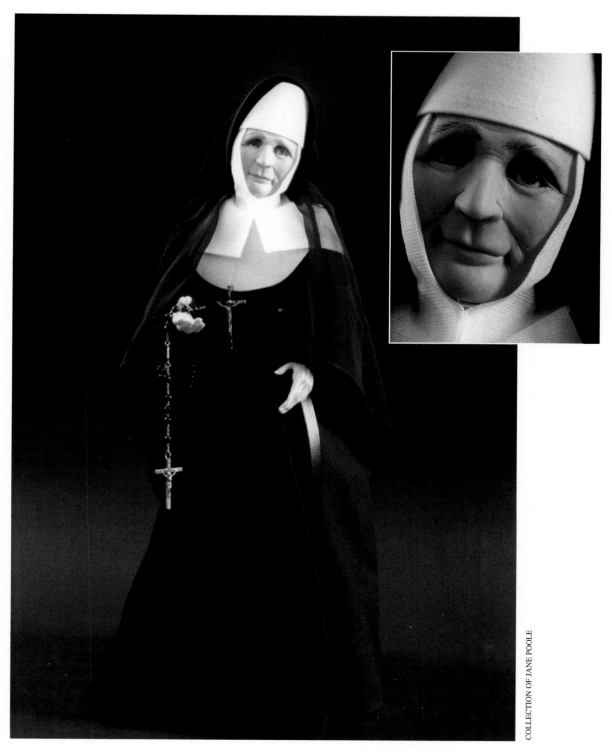

The Nun is another one of my favorite dolls. The face of **The Nun** is that of my mother. The doll is kept in my mother's collection and is her favorite doll. I actually made two Nun dolls from Creall Therm that are very much alike; the second was auctioned off to raise money for the Children's Miracle Network. The winning bidder, who got the piece for $1,600, was Sharon Calabrese of New Baltimore, Michigan.

I was asked to make a Santa Claus for the *Modern Masters* television program for HGTV. The camera crew filmed over my shoulder while I make the complete Santa for the program. It took approximately twelve hours to sculpt the doll and five minutes to show the process on television. I call this figure the **HGTV Santa**, because it is featured each Christmas season on the HGTV series, *Modern Masters*.

I once decided to hand make a leather saddle to fit one of my dolls, and created this sad **Cowboy with Saddle**, 14 inches seated, from Cernit. The old cowboy made the saddle for his little granddaughter, but she passed away before she could ever use it. We can just imagine what is going through his mind as he ponders his loss.

I have a lot of fun sculpting dolls, but making the **Crow Warrior Ready for Battle** was one of the most enjoyable experiences I've ever had making a doll. I researched his costume and made all of his accessories by hand, including a bow and arrow that really shoot. Everything on the doll is made from natural resources; the 20-inch doll is made from ProSculpt.

One of my very first dolls was this **Boat Builder**. I photographed him on his porch with a hammock in the background. Even though the hammock was life-size, it was photographed in such a way as to look like it was in scale with the doll. He is 14-inches, seated, and made from Cernit.

About the same time that I made the **Boat Builder** I made the **Old Salt Fisherman**. I photographed him on the pier in Sarasota, Florida, and his surroundings helped to bring this character to life. His hat and sweater were made from a pair of knit socks. He is made from Cernit, and is 14 inches, seated.

I did a series of black musicians, all known as **The Jazz Player**, beginning with the figure above left, which was made for the 1991 National Institute of American Doll Artists convention in New Orleans. He is made from Cernit. The "Post No Bills" version, above right, was made from Creall Therm, just for fun, in 1995. Both dolls are 14 inches, seated.

This rendition of **The Jazz Player,** 20 inches, won a nomination for the *Dolls* Awards of Excellence at the 1999 American International Toy Fair in New York City. New York City seemed like a fitting place for him. One of the first dolls ever made from ProSculpt, he went on to be a cover doll for *Contemporary Doll* magazine in 2000.

The Fan, 17 inches, made from Creall Therm, was inspired by an old-timer we saw at a ball game. Some of my best ideas come out of my daily life experiences. I rarely go anywhere that I don't see someone worth sculpting. I will never run out of ideas as long as there is a ball game to attend, or a bus or an airplane to ride on.

At the same time as I found the airplane for my **Aviator**, I found this push-car fire engine. It seemed like a good backdrop for a black doll I was working on, **Tara Jane**.

I decided to make the doll if for no other reason than that the red and yellow of the car looked good with the butterfly in her hand and the flower on her hat.

Once when I was teaching a dollmaking seminar in Iowa the students thought it would be appropriate for me to make my take on Grant Wood's famous *American Gothic* painting. Rather than worry about copyright, I just made the couple look like people out of my imagination. It just so happened they had on new shoes, so I named the piece **New Shoes**.

Nana, 14 inches, seated, has always been one of my favorites, and the favorite of so many who enjoy my work. She was fashioned from Cernit after my own grandmother. I remember that when she taught me to sew, I thought it was a waste of my time, but interestingly enough I spend much of my time sewing nowadays. Thanks to my grandmother, I'm not bad at it.

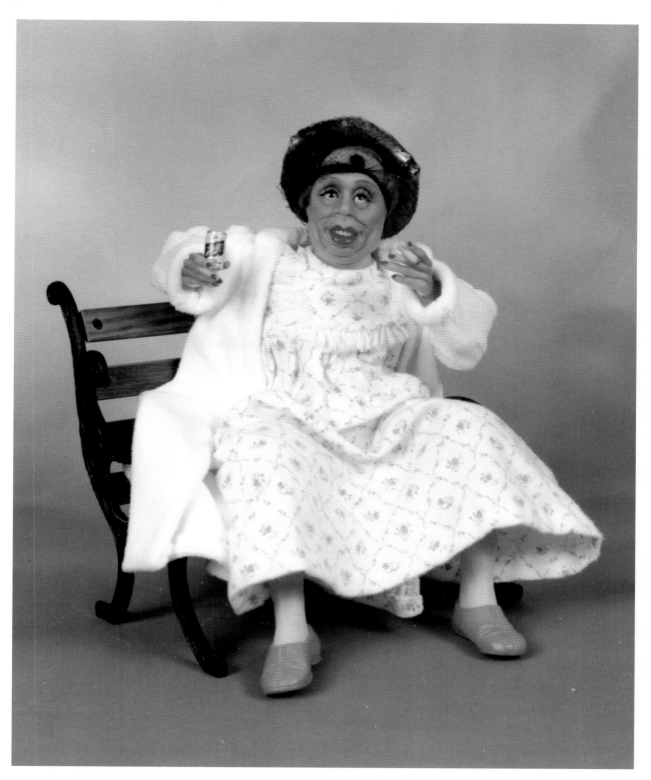

I once had a student who started her day with a cigarette and a can of beer. Her name will remain a secret, but the doll I made in commemoration of her habit is called **So How Do You Start Your Morning**. She is 12 inches, seated, and made from Cernit.

Every February when we go to New York City for Toy Fair I make a new Santa to bring a little Christmas joy to our lives. Once I saw a Santa tap dancing on Broadway for what ever the audience threw to him. It seemed like a great sculpt, so here is my **Broadway Santa**, 14 inches, and made from Creall Therm.

Darcella solves the problem of using a doll stand by never needing one—she is always sitting down. Notice that she is leaning on her own hands, which makes her very stable. Her upturned gaze and laughing mouth suggest the presence of other characters in her story. She is 9 inches, seated, and made from Cernit.

After 35 years this character is **Still Cool**, so that's what I named him. He hasn't out grown his life style or his bad habits. Sculpting his hand making the peace sign was easily accomplished by using an armature inside the hand. Sculpted from ProSculpt, he stands 18 inches high.

The Ship Builder, 14 inches, seated, is another of my favorite sculptures. His costume, hair, beard and the ship in the bottle speak volumes about his life at sea.

While sculpting this very simple doll, I couldn't help wondering what he might be reminiscing about. He is made from ProSculpt.

Native American braves and warriors of the west all went through a time of fasting and praying to receive a name and direction, which was known as the **Vision Quest**. This was a very spiritual experience of asking for guidance. They often spent several days, some-times even weeks, without food and water until the vision came to them. A beautiful **Princess** brought this brave his name and his answer. Notice there is only one set of tracks leading to the scene; she is part of his vision. The 17-inch dolls are made from Cernit.

The Medicine Man, 12 inches, kneeling, is made entirely from natural resources. His head covering is the skin of a small rodent. His deerskin costume is hand sewn and glued. Photographing him in the wilderness, in a pose of prayer, added to his realism. His stone hammer is made from polymer clay.

Gallery of Dolls — 137

Once Santa brought me a new Columbia bike just like the one used in this sculpture. It was such a thrill to find this accessory that I had to make a Santa to go with it. As is the case with many of my sculptures, I made the doll to fit the accessory. Then I named the piece **Santa with Jack's bike**. Santa is made from ProSculpt and stands 9 inches tall.

The two dolls shown on this page represent my development as a sculptor. **Father Christmas**, above left, was sculpted from Cernit in 1990 and was the first doll I ever made. He is in ¾ human scale. The life-size **Santa**, above and top right, was sculpted of ProSculpt in 2002. Studying these two dolls is evidence that time and practice do make a difference.

Glossary of Dollmaking Terms

Adult Goat: An Angora goat that is three or more years old is considered an adult. Its fiber ranges from curly to straight and is low luster. This is the age at which the longest lengths can grow on these goats, as the fiber does not felt on the coat as readily. To achieve lengths of seven-to-ten-inch mohair, the coat must grow on the animal for nine to 14 months. It is very hard to keep clean and matte-free, and brings a very high market price.

Alpaca and Llama: The staple of this shorn or brushed fiber ranges from two to eight inches in length. It is a soft, low-luster fiber with no lanolin, and is often more dusty and grassy than wool and mohair. Llama fiber has no crimp, yet some Surri Alpaca fiber does. This luxury fiber brings a very high market piece, and is often combed with wool into a roving to make it more affordable on the market. In order to achieve longer lengths, the farmer must care for the coats for one to three years. Some of the endangered sheep breeds grow nearly identical fiber in 12 months, and in 27 colors as well. These cousins offer a variety of white, tan, brown, black and gray fibers for dollmakers to enjoy using in trims, yarn embellishments, and any other areas where the characteristics match the inspiration.

Angora Rabbit: Depending upon the breed of Angora, the fiber is from one-half to four inches in length. Angora fiber has no lanolin, and is very soft. It does not have crimps in it. Shorn fiber can be used without harming the animal. It may be used as accent trims in costuming and on toys and props in dollmaking creations. It is a luxury fiber, and so it is hard to find ranches that can raise the fiber to be of consistently good quality fiber. As a result, it brings a high market price.

Body Stocking: The doll body is made from fabric that is shaped and sewn into a body stocking. The fabric body covers a metal frame or armature for the doll. The body stocking is then stuffed firmly with polyfill to create the shape of a doll's body.

Camel fiber: This fiber is primarily available in a soft tan color. Camels are a dual-coated animal, and the fiber has both soft down and very scratchy guard hair. A mix of down and guard hair roving is be more affordable than the de-haired down. The tan-colored fiber is very difficult to find in mohair and wool, so camel fibers are very appealing.

Cotton Roving: This roving can be used to braid rugs for base props or for braided hair on dolls. It is generally used on cloth dolls, but can give a unique look on polymer or porcelain doll too. Naturally colored cotton is raised in the United States. There was considerable controversy during the 1990s about keeping it on the market because the white-cotton industry put great pressure on the naturally colored-cotton industry.

Cure: To cure a polymer doll means to harden the clay in an oven. Often the terms firing or baking the doll are used synonymously with curing, however, the true term is curing.

Firing: See above. The term firing comes from the ancient kilns that were actually heated with fire from wood or coal. Today kilns are heated with gas or electricity. The term firing is still used and is considered proper.

Fleece: This is the product that comes off sheep and goats at harvest time when the animals are shorn (hair cut). Shearing of the flock happens biannually or annually, depending upon the breed of the animal and the use intended for the fiber.

Grommet: The grommet, or eyelet, as it is sometimes called, is a small brass eye that is sewn or pressed into fabric as an anchoring point for string or rope to be tied into the cloth. Small grommets are placed into polymer clay to resemble shoelace holes. They may be seen in Chapter 5, Sculpting the Feet and Shoes.

Horsehair Brush: This five-inch-long tool is made to assist the sculptor in putting wrinkles into the face of a polymer doll. It is made from a horse's tail.

Kid Mohair: This is the virgin clip (first harvest) from an Angora goat that is no more than one year old. It is very fine, lustrous and curly. This fiber brings the highest market price.

Ladder Stitch: The ladder stitch is often called the hidden stitch. It is used to sew up a seam without showing the thread. This stitch is shown in the Chapter 6, Creating the Soft-Sculpted Body. It was taught to me by Gloria "Mimi" Winer.

Living Hide: This is a fleece that has been shorn off the live animal. The clipped side of the hair is felted, and the sheet of hair is left intact to form a pelt. (No harm has come to the animal.)

Locks: These are the individual curls that come from the separated fleece.

Mohair: This fiber comes from the Angora goat. It grows in white, tan, gray and black. Colored fiber can be rare, especially in the tan range. The longer the fiber, the more expensive the mohair. Mohair ranges from high to low luster, and varies from tight curls to straight locks, depending upon the age of the animal it comes from. It is popular in dollmaking for hair and beards and dyes very nicely. Mohair is much harder to work with than wool.

One-of-a-kind series: These two terms together seem to be an oxymoron, however there is such a thing. The term refers to a group of ten to 20 dolls that are each created as one-of-a-kinds, but are nearly identical. A good example of this phenomenon outside of the doll world is the Santa Claus that appears in nearly every department store during the Christmas season, All are Santas, yet no two are exactly alike, and thus they are each one-of-a-kind. To be a one-of-a-kind, each doll must be hand made and different in appearance from any other doll. No two one-of-a-kind dolls, even in a series, are exactly the same.

Pelt/Hide: Wool or mohair that is still on the tanned skin is considered a pelt or hide. The animal is no longer living. Pelts and hides are used in dollmaking for hair, beards and clothing.

Plate of Mohair: This is a plate of animal hair or fiber that is left on the skin. Animal hair such as a goat, sheep, llama, or lamb is left on the skin and tanned into a hide. The plate is then used to make clothing for humans, dolls or for other similar purposes. The plates are also used to make wigs for dolls.

Prototype: One special reproduction doll is made after the master sculpture is complete. This doll is generally made of resin from a mold of the original. The prototype is eventually used to create the master mold. The prototype doll does not have hair, paint or costuming. If it is being reproduced in porcelain, resin or vinyl, its body parts are sanded and refined to perfection, then cleaned and given to the mold maker. The artist who makes the prototype for reproduction must be a fine craftsperson.

Pounce Wheel: This is a special tool used to make

pounce patterns into wet polymer clay. The tool has a small wheel of tiny teeth laying end to end. When rolled on wet polymer clay, it leaves indentation marks that resemble sewn stitches.

Proportion Wheel: The proportion wheel is a measuring device designed into a wheel. It works much as a slide rule does in mathematics. This simplified wheel shows the size relationships for all of the various limbs and body parts of a sculpted doll.

Polyfill: Acrylic fibers spun into a ball are used for stuffing dolls, teddy bears, etc. Polyfill has, for the most part, replaced cotton as a filling agent.

Raw Fiber: This refers to unwashed fleeces from an animal.

Roving Wool: This can be wool or mohair that has been brushed on a drum carder so that the fibers are aligned into a long tube, which can range from thin to thick. Roving wool or mohair is used in dollmaking for hair, costuming, braided rugs and accessories.

Silk Fiber: Silk is a wonderful protein fiber that comes in many useful forms. A doll artist can make use of silk cocoons, caps, top, noil, waste, yarn and fabric. It takes on dye in the most vibrant and magical way, lending luster to costuming, moth and butterfly doll wings, trims, stained glass looks and a multitude of other looks.

3-in-1 Tool: The 3-in-1 primary sculpting tool was designed by Jack Johnston and manufactured by the Kemper Tool Company of Chino California. The three tools in one consist of a primary sculpting tool, an ear tool and a fingernail tool.

Tumbling: This machine process is used on raw fiber to help release the grass and dirt from the fiber before it is washed.

Wefting: Wefting mohair is the process of sewing mohair together into a long strand of hair in preparation for making a wig. Wefting is thought of as the highest and best use of mohair. Only the finest mohair is wefted.

Wipeout Tool: This tool is specifically made to remove paint from a porcelain or polymer sculpture. It has rubber ends formed in the shape of a wedge. The rubber wedges look very much like erasers of the end of a pencil.

Wool: Fiber from any breed of sheep is considered wool. It grows in as many as 27 natural colors, depending upon the breed of the sheep. Endangered sheep breeds widen the range of choices significantly. The locks range from two to 18 inches, low to high luster, crimped, curly wispy or wavy, again depending upon the breed. Sheep are shorn every four to 12 months.

Yearling clip: The fiber from an adolescent Angora goat, one to two years of age, it is still curly and lustrous.

Sources

Suppliers

Most of the tools, materials and supplies described in this book can be purchased at crafts and hobby stores nationwide, or from specific websites that serve dollmakers. Several major retail chains also have websites, listed below, through which you can either order supplies, or find the locations of the branch nearest you

Hobby Lobby
www.hobbylobby.com

Jane's Original Artdoll Supplies
800-560-4958
www.janesdollsupplies.com

Joann Fabrics
800-525-4951
www.joann.com

Johnston Original Artdolls
800-290-9998
www.artdolls.com

Michaels Arts and Crafts
www.michaels.com

Pearl Art, Craft & Discount Art Center
www.pearlart.com

Artist Organizations and Guilds

Academy of American Doll Artists (AADA)
This group was founded in 1994 to promote original artist dolls as an art form. Among its educational and marketing purposes, it aims to provide economical marketing opportunities to its artists.
603-226-4501
www.aadadoll.org

National Institute of American Doll Artists (NIADA)
Now an international organization, NIADA was formed in 1963 for the purpose of promoting the original, handmade doll. Membership standards are high; collectors are also accepted as patron members.
www.niada.org

Original Doll Artists Council of America (ODACA)
Founded in 1976 as an artists' organization, ODACA provides educational opportunities and conferences. AUX-ODACA was organized in 1981 to promote American original artists and their work.
www.odaca.org

The Professional Doll Makers Art Guild (PDMAG)
In 1992 I asked my first 13 professional students to join with me in forming an art guild and go to Toy Fair in New York. This was the foundation of the PDMAG in 1993, which has the goal of assisting those who want to become professional dollmakers. It is now an international organization.
800-290-9998
www.artdolls.com

United Federation of Doll Clubs (UFDC)

Now an international organization made up of doll clubs throughout the country and abroad, the UFDC was founded in 1949. Devoted to the study and enjoyment of dolls, UFDC includes thousands of collectors, as well as artists, among its members.
816-891-7040
www.ufdc.org

Publications and Web Sites

There are numerous magazines and web sites serving both dollmakers and doll collectors. All can be contacted via the internet, at the following addresses.

Contemporary Doll Collector
www.scottpublications.com

Doll Artisan
Doll Costuming
Doll Crafter
Dollmaking
Dolls
www.jonespublishing.com

Doll Reader
www.dollreader.com

www.dollmagazine.com
www.dollshowmagazine.com
www.virtualdolls.com

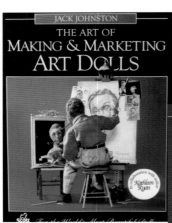

Books

We have come a long way since aspiring dollmakers looked in vain for books to help them in their education. Many excellent books have been published on various kinds of dollmaking, from cloth to porcelain to polymer clays.

My first published book was entitled *The Art of Making and Marketing Artdolls.* It was a great success in assisting artists to learn to make and market their dolls. It also provided a great service as a supplement to my seminars and videos. My second book, *The Advanced Art of Making and Marketing Artdolls* was, as the title suggests, aimed at the more advanced student. Both books were published by Scott Publications and are now out of print. Some retailers still have a few copies on sale.

A few other books that I believe are especially useful include the following.

Armstrong-Hand, Martha. *Learning to be a Doll Artist.* Livonia, Michigan: Scott Publications, 1999.

Gunzel, Hildegard. *Creating Original Porcelain Dolls.* Cumberland, MD: Hobby House Press, 1989.

Lichtenfels, Lisa. *Figures in Fabric: The Sculpture of Lisa Lichtenfels.* Cumberland, Maryland: Portfolio Press, 2001.

McKinley, Robert. *Dollmaking, One Artist's Approach.* Richmond, Virginia: William Byrd Press, 1991.

Oroyan, Susanna. *Anatomy of a Doll.* Lafayette, California: C&T Publishing, 1997.

Oroyan, Susanna. *Designing the Doll.* Lafayette, California: C&T Publishing, 1999.

Oroyan, Susanna. *Fantastic Figures.* Lafayette, California: C&T Publishing, 1994.